FALLEN, FELON, *and finally* FAITH

Autobiography

of

Dr. Ralph R. Reagan

Written by Ralph Reagan, ThD, with Mary Greene

Book cover contributed by Jon Weaver

Liaison work by Paul Leighty

Dedication

This book is dedicated to my patient and long-suffering wife, Connie. She had faith when I didn't.

It's also dedicated to my mother, now passed away. She suffered untold hardships, and I was one of them.

Acknowledgements

Thanks to Mary Greene, copy editor, who also taped and transcribed portions of editions One and Two of the book, contributed parts of the book, and formatted the book for printing.

Also, thanks to Collene Martin for taping and transcribing portions of my story for the first edition.

Second Edition
Published by

Miracle on Fourth Street Press
281 Fourth Street
Crossville, TN 38555-4304

Printed by

Lightning Source, Inc.
an Ingram Company
1246 Heil Quaker Blvd
La Vergne, TN 37086

Book Cover Design by

Jon Weaver
Crossville, Tennessee

ISBN: 978-0-9672791-6-9 (April 2008)

ISBN: 978-0-9672791-5-2 (October 2010)

Fallen, Felon, *and finally* Faith

The autobiography of Dr. Ralph Reagan

Introduction

Due to the overwhelming response to the first edition of this book, we decided to update it to include news of the on-going ministries, numerous miracles, and expanding facilities.

Testimonials have come in from prisoners all over the country—letting Ralph know how his story has inspired them. We hope it will continue to do so.

Mary Greene
October 2010

§§§§

Ralph Randall Reagan

Committed — to Rebellion
Committed — to Reform School
Committed — to Organized Crime
Committed – to Prison

▯▯▯▯

Committed — to Christ
Committed to acquiring a Theological Education
Committed — to a Ministry for the Homeless
Committed — to a Prison Ministry

Ralph Reagan surely is a man of commitment.

A drunk at the age of nine, in reform school and prison by the age of thirteen, scared witness to his friend's murder at thirteen, involved with a murder while in his early twenties, given up for dead after a drunken car wreck, on Organized Crime's "hit list" in his late teens, another death warrant for violating a prison code—a real loser his whole life—and a new Christian beginning a new life in his late twenties.

In 2009, Ralph completed his Doctor of Theology (ThD). He continues his commitment to the homeless, the destitute and the prison population—and to anyone without Christ. He travels far and wide on their behalf.

What lies between Ralph Reagan's birth and his present-day life is astonishing to say the least. The very fact that he is alive proves that two thousand years after a wedding in Cana, miracles are still occurring. Ralph Reagan, by all accounts, should not even be alive today, much less managing the rescue mission he founded and preaching to homeless and destitute souls on a daily basis.

If you don't believe in miracles now, you will after reading this account of his life. Nothing less than a miracle could account for his having experienced such a sordid, highly-dangerous life, then experiencing a 180-degree turnaround. The good being done in this world now by Ralph Reagan is beyond belief—but, believe it.

Ralph has revealed this information about his past life for one purpose only—to help others overcome past failures and discover how sweet life can be. He especially wants those in prison to know there is hope for everyone who will accept Jesus Christ into their lives and accept forgiveness for past sins. Ralph himself is living proof of this.

Even as a young teenager, Ralph knew that Christ was trying to reach him. But, he couldn't "let go and let God." This book tells of his extraordinary experiences during the intervening years before he finally had a life-changing experience while in prison.

Ralph serves on the Community Resources Board at the Southeastern Tennessee State Regional Correctional Facility (STSRCF), Pikeville. Working with the warden, chaplain and others, he is helping to expand the role of volunteers to mentor and tutor inmates in all phases of life skills needed to cope when they are released. Without such a program, many inmates will find themselves victims of "the revolving door." Helping inmates manage emotional and social skills by teaching them such simple items as how to communicate socially, manage a bank account, control anger and discouragement, manage stress, and other seemingly routine skills restores their self-esteem and starts them on the road to becoming good citizens. Without such a program, many inmates will find themselves victims of "the revolving door." He wants them to know that God loves *them* just as much as He does everyone else.

Ralph gives all the credit for each success story to the Holy Spirit working through him and others.

After working with Ralph on this autobiography, I felt compelled to interview his wife, Connie, for further information about herself and the Bread of Life Rescue Mission. Her story appears in the back of the book, after Ralph's. Connie hopes this will help readers to better understand the needs and purposes of the rescue mission.

Some older people find it hard to accept the fact that Ralph is no longer the "low life" he once was. Believe me, if you heard Ralph give his testimony or followed him around for a day or two, you would know that this man truly is a changed man. He is a man of God. He is God's man. If he didn't tell you of his past, you would never, never imagine Ralph as a criminal. He loves the Lord, and he loves his fellow man—no matter what the circumstances. (It would be hard to find anyone who has endured worse circumstances than Ralph himself, so he truly knows how to empathize.) Anyone who doubts is invited to visit the Bread of Life Rescue Mission in Crossville, Tennessee.

It has been a privilege to assist Ralph and Connie with this book. It also has been a privilege to get to know these two remarkable people and the many others associated with and furthering the cause of the Bread of Life Rescue Mission—doctors, lawyers, former inmates, alcoholics in remission, and people from every walk of life.

Boy! Talk about miracles...!

Mary Greene
April 2008

Hope for the Hopeless
The Miracle on Fourth Street

Chapter 1

Ralph the Boy

Reverend Ralph Reagan knelt in prayer before he began telling his life story to Collene Martin, who was taping it.

He asked that God lead him in remembering and telling his story. He asked that God make his testimony an instrument to touch someone's life.

He asked God to touch hearts and lives through his testimony.

Ralph's desire is that others may come to know Christ and His saving knowledge, and know the reality of God's love and the difference it can make in their lives.

* * * * * * *

This is his story

My father would often come in drunk and be abusive to my mother. I remember the fighting and the smell of alcohol on my father. I remember my mother's tears and how helpless I felt because I was so little.

When I was four years old, my mother finally divorced my father. My father's leaving is just a vague memory. My mom and dad had a fight, and she ran him off.

After the fights, separation, and finally divorce, my mom, my nine brothers and sisters, and I moved out of a rented house into a little old tarpaper house on the same road in Crossville, Tennessee.

Our house was small and frail, but it filled the bill. It had thin walls, and the wind whistled through the cracks in the winter. The roof leaked, and you could poke holes in the walls to ventilate it in the summertime. The house had two bedrooms, a living room, back porch, front porch and outdoor plumbing. There was a well out behind the house. There was lots of room for growing kids to run. The road was about 75 feet away from the front porch.

But, there was never any time to sit and listen to the crickets or visit with each other. However, the whole point is that we were together. We were a family. My mom loved us all, and she was taking a stand. She was making a new life for us kids. She didn't want to be hurt anymore, and she didn't want us to go through the pushing and shoving and cowering of the angry, drunken sprees of my dad.

My mother would do odd jobs: washing, ironing, and cleaning for other people to make money to see to our needs. She was constantly working and always striving for a better life for her ten children. She was home just long enough to cook and clean—taking care of our bodily needs.

It was a time that my mother just barely made ends meet. There was never much food in the house, but she saw to it that we never went to bed hungry. She always had something there for us to eat. I remember biscuits and gravy was one of my favorite foods. (Still is.) It was hard times, but we made it through.

My mom swallowed her pride and applied to move into the housing projects so her children could have a good home. She had a plan. She was going on with her life and taking care of her babies. She was strong-willed and

2

determined to make it. Mother didn't know the words "quit" or "give up."

(It just so happens that where those housing projects were is directly behind and two doors down from the new Bread of Life Rescue Mission. It's as if God has sent me right back to my starting point. This time we'll get it right. God surely knows, doesn't He!)

The projects were the first home we had ever lived in that had a bathroom inside. My mother applied for a job at the Cumberland Mountain Farm Bakery. She got the job and walked four miles to work through rain, sleet or snow. It seemed that it didn't much matter to her, but she would always try to keep things going at the house for us. She felt the burden to see that we had food on the table, clothes on our backs, and shoes on our feet.

She saw to it that we got our school homework done. She would always fix supper for us no matter how tired she was; our needs came first. Time was not a hindrance or matter of question when it came to her children. She was up early to go to work to provide for us, and in bed late, after caring for her children. She saw to it that we were full and snug in our beds. There were no sugar plums dancing in our heads, but we were taken care of.

My mother was a very pretty woman, a hard worker with a big heart. She had long hair and blue eyes. She was a very well-built lady. But she carried a heavy load. She would have it no other way. She had a caring heart that loved her children, and she worked long, hard days.

If any of my brothers' friends, or my friends, came in hungry, there was always enough beans and cornbread or biscuits and gravy to go around. If any one of them needed a place to stay, there was always enough room.

3

But there was a constant gnawing feeling in me that I was a burden to her. I longed to be able to take some of the pain and some of the load off her shoulders. This boy, so small, watched as she worked tirelessly for all of us. I saw this woman work eight, ten or twelve hours a day—there was no limit to her labor of love.

Because of my mother being a single parent who had to work long hours, we grew up with no authority in the home. There were three girls and seven boys who all grew up together. She never wanted us kids to be separated.

We never had anybody to tell us what to do or what *not* to do. With all the hours she had to work, she was not able to give us twenty-four-hour care. There wasn't enough of her to go around. So, she did all she knew to do, work and love us, being mother and father as much as possible.

Well, all the boys would just run around and do whatever they wanted; especially me. Staying in town was a major occurrence. My time in town was spent hanging around picking up Coke bottles in the evenings to buy milk and books needed for school. In my mind, I was helping the only way I knew how.

Several people in town at restaurants and filling stations bought my returnable Coke bottles. They'd let me come in and hang around.

This was when I started having trouble with the law. The town had a curfew to keep us kids out of trouble, and we would always try to stay out past the curfew just to get the policemen to run after us. It was sort of a game; it gave us a thrill just doing anything to upset the police officers.

At about nine or ten years old, my hangouts were the beer joints in Crossville. The people liked me and bought me sodas. One of the guys who owned a beer joint offered me a job cleaning up around there to earn some

4

money. I said I would, and I began working for him. A couple of dollars was enough to pay for my milk and school supplies.

One Sunday, because the beer joint was not allowed to be open on Sunday, the owner locked me in to do my chores. I was mopping the floor and cleaning up when I decided to steal and drink my first beer.

That was a day never to be forgotten. That beer was a Black Label, and it took a can opener to open it. I sure felt big opening that can. It was as if I had some kind of power. I felt kind of grown up. That beer was the best thing this boy had ever tasted in his life.

When Buster, the boss, came in and realized that I had drunk a beer, he just laughed about it. He didn't give me any warning or tell me to stop. It was just funny to him. From that time on, I drank constantly. There was nothing and nobody to stop me.

One thing led to another.

Some of my older friends and I would go out and steal because we couldn't afford the beer. Our pastime was breaking into stores and doing whatever we could to try to accumulate money to buy more beer.

All of us, my friends and I, would even go up to the front of the Kroger store and hand notes to elderly people saying that our Dad was home sick in bed with alcoholism, and we needed to get him some medicine.

The old folks would take pity on us and play right into our hands, giving us money. My older brother would buy the beer because we were too young to buy alcohol. He'd bring it out and give it to us, and we would take it home and drink it. Our effort was put into doing everything we could to get it. We even began breaking into the beer joints.

5

Of course, by this time, I was having a real struggle in school. I struggled with my studies and with the attitudes of the other kids.

One morning, I wore a pair of pants to school that my mother had mended. When she sewed them up, it left a noticeable patch. I had to go to the front of the class, and, as I returned to my seat, the other kids began to laugh and make fun of my patched pants. When they started to laugh at me that day, I turned to walk through the door and purposed in my heart never to go back to that school.

Chapter 2

Hard Lessons

After the incident at school, I started going to Raymond Atkins' house—my home away from home—instead of going to school. We'd ride around in the park, or there was an old house where we'd hang out and sit around all day. We were drinking, killing time, doing nothing until time to go home, as if we had been in school all day.

One day, Raymond was out riding horses. I wasn't there at the time, but just about any other time, we'd have been together. The horse he was riding began to buck, and Raymond was in some serious trouble. The horse tried to scrape him off on an old wood fence and cut him good on a nail sticking out from one of the old boards. It ripped Raymond's leg half off, and he lost quite a bit of blood. When someone finally found him, they took him to the hospital.

After this happened, we were both put in jail for truancy. Our hanging-out days came to an abrupt halt. We were both thirteen at the time.

We were placed in jail with a man named Big John. He was in jail for killing his stepchildren. He had thrown them down a well. We couldn't help but wonder why Big John had done it and what he might do if he got mad at us. Whispering in the night, we tried to figure out what would happen and what could we do if he did get mad at us. Here we were in a jail cell with a man who had killed his stepchildren, and the sheriff had put this killer in charge of us.

The sheriff told John to talk to us and take care of us. The sheriff said, "These here boys don't want to listen to their parents. Now, you just give 'em a good talkin' to, John, and maybe they'll listen."

John never bothered us. He really never did say much of anything to us. He pretty well stayed on his side of the cell and paid the two of us no mind. He seemed to have a lot on his mind.

Then came the day of judgment. Judge Horn was the judge presiding at that time, and from court, we went to reform school for truancy. I was thirteen years old.

The reform school was like nowhere we'd ever been before. It was in Nashville. We were country boys. We were scared. I can remember the fear of where we were going and what we might face each day. The sheriff and deputies in Crossville had us pumped full of stories, and we were pretty much afraid of our shadows by the time we got there to that big city.

It was the big city for two young boys, but no sightseeing.

There, we had our first encounter with racism, a new experience. Crossville was a little town nestled on the Cumberland Plateau. There were no blacks and no knowledge of or interaction with blacks.

About three months after we got there, Raymond got into a fight with a boy named Webster, a young black man. Raymond won the fight, and he felt like he had whipped Webster real good.

That few moments of victory was short-lived. We were really about to learn a hard lesson in life.

8

The supervisor of the reform school was a big black man. He said, "Every time we have folks here from Crossville, we have this problem."

The supervisor took Raymond into the bathroom and beat him that night. He beat him bad. Whenever they finally came out, Raymond just barely made it to his bed.

We all stood at attention beside our beds there in the dormitory while the bathroom incident was going on. We heard it all, loud and clear, the blows and the words. I had a sick feeling in the pit of my stomach. I wanted to be real sick. The Supervisor told the rest of us to go on to bed.

The next morning, Raymond's nose, ears and lips were purple. That morning, we went out to formation after breakfast. Formation was a place like a military setting. Each one would stand there in line until they called us out to go to work or sessions.

Well, Raymond fell out to go to the hospital. He was beaten so badly that his heart was leaking blood. A lonely feeling gripped me—an almost numb feeling—as I watched him limp away to the hospital. Raymond died several days later.

I got out about the time that Raymond died. I went to his funeral to say goodbye to a childhood friend. A little bit of me seemed to die with him.

My anger at the world's injustices in life grew. I just did not understand why Raymond was killed. It began to really take hold and boil inside of me. Raymond's death just added fuel to the rebellion that was already there. It was a low flame that had just been turned up a couple of notches.

I did have thoughts about God, but I just did not understand.

9

Chapter 3

The Carnival

Since Raymond's death, I had already been sent back to reform school for "Breaking and Entering."

By now, there was a little more crust on my heart, and I had a little more know-how of the ins and outs of things.

Me and a couple of my real good friends, Bobby and Billy Flynn, had broken into a couple of stores. Anything we could do to get the things we wanted, we did it. We saw that all the other kids had things and figured the only way we would get stuff was to steal. We did anything, always on the edge.

During this time, my mother was working constantly to pay the bills and keep things going. I didn't realize what I was doing to my mother. From the time I could remember, she was always working, and I felt like a problem, a burden, a hindrance. I thought that if it were not for me, she would not have to work so hard. I was always trying to do something for my mother, because of that gnawing feeling in the pit of my stomach that I was trouble for her.

If I stole something, I took the money I got from selling it to my mother. But my mother would never accept the gifts of money from stolen goods. At the same time, she never hid me from the police when they would come for me. She had always tried to teach us to do right, but we just would not listen. She was an honest woman and always wanted to make a good, clean, honest living. She tried to teach each of us children those same principles.

I kept trying to find places to go so I wouldn't be a burden to her. I wasn't doing right, but the anger on the inside drove me on. I had mixed emotions. I wanted what I wanted, yet I didn't want to hurt my mother. I was torn between those two options, but hardheadedness and drinking won out.

A carnival came through town when I had just turned fifteen. They set up about two blocks from home.

I lied about my age and went to work there as a laborer. I left home with the carnival. I went to work at the Charlie Brown Glass House for the World of Pleasure. I was paid $21 a week. Everything I had at fifteen years old cost $21 a week.

Another friend of mine, Donnie Owens, went with the carnival too. We got jobs as carnies working on some of the rides or running the games. Donnie only lasted about two months, and he took off.

The most enticing thing about this new job was, if you belonged to the carnival, they would sell you beer. It didn't matter how young you were. You became a member of the family. It was a group of people that would take care of each other. They'd cover each other's back.

There was one big guy named Tiny, a black man. He and his wife took a liking to me and looked out for me. Tiny said that I was just a young, green kid. Tiny made sure that word got out around the carnival to leave me alone. If anyone took my money or stuff, they would have to answer to Tiny. He was, more or less, my self-appointed guardian.

11

So, I just stayed drunk and gambled with them. Got pretty good at gambling too. I won quite a bit of money in the gambling casinos in the carnival. If it were not for Tiny, I probably would have been killed on several occasions for the money I had won in those gambling sessions.

Then, the lifestyle of alcohol and traveling from town to town with the carnival became a horrible existence. I had outlasted my friend Donnie, but, after a year, it finally got to me. Homesickness for my mother and home took over. I had gleaned some more worldly knowledge along the way, but Crossville, Tennessee, was calling me. I had to go.

Chapter 4

From Bad to Worse

A good friend from Coldwater, Michigan, came down and dropped me off in Crossville. I had $61 in my pocket. That was all there was to show for a year's work traveling with the carnival.

Back home in the old stomping grounds, I could still start trouble wherever I went.

The first place I went to was my mother's house. The second place, the beer joint and old friends. The $61 for a year's wages was gone in the blink of an eye.

I was back in jail within a month. The old familiar place hadn't changed since I was twelve years old. It looked the same, smelled the same, and felt the same.

In jail, I met a man named Willard Parks. Willard was in jail for counterfeiting. I had no way of knowing that I was meeting one of the more prominent members of a rather large criminal organization.

The Crossville police had broken up his counterfeiting ring. With it, he had traveled all the way through Florida and up through Tennessee. He had done some traveling.

I gained Willard's trust in jail. I was out in a trusty cell and was able to do things for "Sonny." Willard's nickname was Sonny. Only his friends called him Sonny.

I was doing favors for Sonny, like getting cigarettes and the niceties that he missed from the outside. He took a liking to me, and we became friends.

Sonny told me that if I ever got out of reform school and needed work, for me to get in touch. He said that he'd be out in a couple of days, because they didn't have enough evidence to hold him. So, Sonny promised me a job.

They sent me on to reform school in Pikeville, Tennessee. They sent me to a place they called "a step before prison." It was originally built for black people. In the early 50's, they kept the blacks and whites separate. They didn't start to integrate the reform schools and prisons until the 60's and 70's. I had just turned seventeen years old when I went there in 1972.

I really had a rough time there. They caught me once trying to escape. Then they sent me to Nashville, to a rehab. In Pikeville, I was only about twenty miles from my home. They wanted to get me farther away from my hometown of Crossville.

They sent me to a rehab center right next to the main prison in Nashville for nine months. I went through rehab and ended up right back in Crossville again. I didn't have anywhere else to go.

I kept wanting to work but couldn't find a job. Suddenly, I remembered what Sonny had told me, and I gave him a call. Sonny came to pick me up for a visit.

Sonny asked me what I could do, and my reply was, "I don't know how to do mucha nothin'."

Sonny said, "If you'll be down here tomorrow, you can go to work for me."

I responded with, "I don't have any way to get there." At that time, I wasn't at my mama's house; I was some distance from home. I had no transportation to get that far away—or much of anywhere, for that matter.

14

Sonny scratched his head and said, "Well, if you'll get you some clothes from your mother's, we'll just go on down there to my house." Sonny always seemed to have the answers.

He took me by my mama's house, and I quickly threw together what few clothes I had. I didn't want to keep him waiting; he had me a job.

I went to Sonny's house; met his wife and his children. I just moved in with them and became part of Sonny's family.

Chapter 5

The Lady with the Piercing Green Eyes

At seventeen, I went to work at a rock quarry that Sonny leased. Sonny showed me how to work the rock. It was hard work.

Of course, Sonny managed to always keep a case of cold beer around. Sonny drank whiskey, but it hadn't taken him long to know what I liked.

There was something puzzling about Sonny. He would always drop me off and stay gone until time for me to get off work. Lots of questions surrounded his whereabouts during those hours that never got asked out loud, but I figured out some things on my own.

I'd stay with Sonny most of the time, but on the weekends I went home. At home, I would always stay in trouble with one of my brothers. We would fight and argue, and I never really got a chance to be there with my mother. So, I'd head back to Sonny's.

Sonny's home became my home. At this particular time, Sonny, and his wife got into an argument. She left him and took all the children except one son.

The boy's name was David. We got along real good, and I watched David grow up. I'd baby-sit him for Sonny sometimes.

About this time, Sonny started teaching me how to sell whiskey. I was learning how to run whiskey into Crossville, which was in a dry county.

It took quite a while for Sonny to gain a real trust in me; but when he did, I was brought into Sonny's organization.

We did jobs of an illegal nature. Sonny had been doing this for years. He allowed me to go out and do jobs for him that people would pay for.

I didn't see what was coming. I had no idea that I was a pawn in a much larger game. It seems that Sonny was using me. He needed people to go out and work for him because he didn't want to get his hands dirty. So, I was one of those up front, handy guys.

I had never really had a dad, and Willard was somewhere around fifty. He seemed to fill the bill. I looked up to him, but didn't realize how much I was being used.

Sonny would do just about anything for me that I asked him to do. That made me feel really important. Sonny would give me beer or loan me money, keeping me satisfied. He never would allow me enough money that I could leave though. Sonny always owed me money. He never allowed me to have my full pay. He always owed me just enough to keep me where he wanted me. He was shrewd and an excellent manipulator to get his desired results.

Sonny started opening me up to these jobs. Sonny even began introducing this youngster to members of the gang. They all liked me. It seemed as though all the members of this organized crime syndicate liked me. They told Sonny they had some jobs to do and set it up for me to go on the road with them.

Before this time, Sonny had introduced me to his second-cousin Connie. Well, he didn't exactly introduce me—he dared me to go in and kiss his cousin.

I said, "Why sure!"

It was September 11, her sixteenth birthday.

17

I walked right in and found this beautiful green-eyed girl with a towel wrapped around her head. She had just washed her hair. When she took that towel off, I saw she had the most beautiful, dark brown, curly hair you've ever seen.

There I stood, tall, slim, and my dark eyes filled with the most gorgeous thing I had ever seen. I had dark hair down to my shoulders, parted on the side. I stood there that day in a T-shirt, jeans and brown jacket with quarry dirt all over me. Boy, for a dare, it turned out real good.

I grabbed her as if I'd known her all my life, kissed her, and ran.

Connie says that very day she knew that I was the man she was going to marry. I didn't see what she saw in me, but she sure was the one for me. She's really stuck by me through the years.

We took to each other. She was some good-looking girl, with the biggest green eyes. I called her "the lady with the piercing green eyes." It didn't take me long to know that she was the one for me.

Connie and I married about fourteen months after we met. We slipped off and didn't tell anyone. Her grandparents and parents, the whole family, were totally against the marriage. My mother didn't have anything to say about it. She was always somewhere else and didn't really have any input. She really didn't get involved; she seemed to feel that it was our business.

After we got married, we moved in with one of the guys that worked for Sonny, because we didn't have a home. I would leave Connie with Sonny and stay gone some two or three weeks at a time. I would bring her money to provide for her and then leave again. I was always on the go and always running. I was too busy to slow down for anything.

18

Chapter 6

A Close Call

Members of the organization would travel from state to state.

In organized crime, some of the people you would work with, not all of them, were officials in the courthouse, the license bureau,—everyday people you would deal with in day-to-day life.

In our travels and dealings, we would go in, set up a business bank account, and the bank would give us a batch of checks for payroll.

A man would go into a new town a week before the other men and I went. They would set up a bogus construction company and make a bank deposit, usually five thousand dollars. They would get those blank payroll checks and run them through from a Friday to a Monday morning. They would throw out as many checks as they could in a weekend. We had blank driver's licenses that we got through our contacts mentioned above, so we made the checks out to fictitious people with fake driver's licenses for identification. They were all bonded company checks.

Then, on Monday morning, a man would go in and draw out all the money except for enough to keep the account open, perhaps five hundred dollars. He told the bank that he would have to go back to the other town they had just left and pick up some other checks to deposit. He would always give the bank president, or whoever he was dealing with, an excuse. He would say something to the effect of, "We have another bank draft coming in either late today or tomorrow." Of course, it never came, and the bank was left holding the bag.

We would leave those towns thousands and thousands of dollars in debt to the bank. We had plenty of money, stayed drunk, and rented the most high-class hotels with the best of food. Everything was only the best money could buy.

During my stay with these people, I was introduced to people who worked in high places, judges, lawyers, a highway patrolman, people who worked with the railroad. I met different people from various walks of life; all were living on the edge. They thought it was exciting doing what they were doing and never being caught. We all lived as if there were no tomorrow—but tomorrow always came.

When I was about twenty-two, my associates and I were in Jasper, Tennessee, five of us, when something went haywire. I had just bought a real nice step-side van and had it pretty well fixed up. It was everything I wanted in a van. It had a CB and an eight-track tape player. It was comfortable.

One Friday evening, I decided to go home to Crossville to see my mother. The guys wanted to use the van in Jasper while I was gone, and I agreed to let them. They had rented a motel room next to the interstate, at the Scottish Inn.

I went on back to Crossville and spent Friday and Saturday night and Sunday morning. The fellows who had given me a ride to Crossville picked me up, and we went back to Jasper together.

A SWAT team was waiting for us when we got there. The policemen had evacuated the whole motel. They had already arrested my associates. As we drove in, we

20

thought things looked sort of funny, but we went to our room anyway. They came in and got us.

It seems that two of the men had gotten too greedy and had gone out and killed a young man. They had kidnapped him, held him for ransom to extort money out of the boy's father, and then killed the boy. The boy's blood was found in the back of my van. One of the boy's motorcycle parts was still there as evidence that they had used the van to dump the body.

They kept me in jail in Jasper for three days. It was proven that I was in Crossville when the killing had taken place, so they released me to a jail in Franklin where I had been in trouble just a few weeks before. They had warrants for my arrest, and they extradited me to Nashville. The charge of robbery was later dropped. (I never did get my van back.)

They had a $5,000 bond on me there in Franklin. One of the members of the organization gave them $5,000 cash to get me out of jail. This was back when $5,000 was quite a bit of money. This man just took it out of his own pocket to get me out of jail. At the time, I thought he was just being my friend, but I realize now he probably was afraid that I might talk.

It wasn't long afterward that I was waiting for trial in a small town outside of Nashville, in White County, Tennessee, and while waiting, several of us got into some more trouble, just small incidents. We were paid to do a particular job in Sparta. There was a lot of corruption going on at that time in that town. There was a very real and present problem among the people. We just did what we were paid to do. I got charged with driving under the influence and carrying a weapon for the purpose of going armed, which they could not prove because they found the weapon *under* my car, not on me.

21

Fallen, Felon, and finally Faith

Chapter 7

Close Brush with Death

From White County, I went to Manchester, Tennessee. One day I went down into this big irrigation system and busted my side. After lying there all night, I finally crawled out, up to a big walkway. I almost died.

Finally, a police officer heard me screaming and got help for me.

At this time, the organization was looking for me. They were in the process of making plans to eliminate me because they thought I had become a liability. This all happened around 1981. By now, I was around twenty-five or twenty-six.

I was in a bar one night, drinking, when an older man approached me. The man asked if I knew any women that might want to make a little money.

I saw my chance at making a little money, so I told the elderly gentleman to sit down, and I would be back in just a few minutes. I knew a girl who would be willing to go along with the man's plans. I went and got her and brought her back to meet this fellow. They hit it off.

Well, I knew I had it made. Every time he bought her a beer, he bought one for me.

After a little time had passed that same evening, we all left together to find a motel room. The old gentleman wanted me to drive.

We found a motel close by, and he rented a room for the night. He told me to take a hike for an hour or two, then come back and pick them up. He gave me a half pint of whiskey and the key to his Jeep. I was on my way. I headed straight over to see my wife, Connie, at her grandmother's house.

By the time I got there, I was so drunk they wouldn't let me come in or around Connie's family.

I got angry, spun my tires, and kicked up a lot of gravel as I sped off. About two miles down the road, I flipped the Jeep seven times. On the second or third flip, I flew out of the Jeep and ended up in a pool of water in a driveway. It was 28 degrees, and there I lay in water nearly freezing. The temperature dipped down colder.

I lay there freezing for over seven hours until a woman going to work the next morning saw the overturned Jeep. I was covered from head to toe with mud and ice. All she could see were my eyes and my nose.

The lady called an ambulance. They picked me up, and when they got me in the hospital, they thought I was already dead.

They called my mother. She came quickly, with a heavy heart. Her son had lain out in this freezing weather for hours. Her mind was racing with memories as to how this could have happened. When she stepped into the hospital room, she couldn't help but cry. She asked the doctors to check me again; she believed I was still breathing.

The main doctor came in and checked me. To his surprise, I was still alive. He quickly gave instructions to cut my clothes off. They stripped me of all my clothes— cutting clothes and boots off inch by inch.

They warmed me up slowly until, after three days,

they decided that I would make it.

No one had stopped to help me when it happened. The people in the house near where the Jeep had turned over did not try to help me. I feel that this was because I had a reputation as a no-good person. They were probably afraid to get involved. They couldn't help but hear the car crash.

By now, nobody liked me, and nobody wanted to help me. To them, I just wasn't worth the effort. I was sarcastic in every way, and I had nothing good to say to anyone. Even when I was in the hospital, people said it would have been better if I had just died. In spite of all the odds against me, something kept me alive. My attitude didn't change—but I lived.

I had been in a coma for three days. I woke up to find three ladies in my room; Connie's aunt and two other ladies from the Church of God of Prophecy from Ravenscroft. They had been praying for me. I said I didn't need their prayers and to get out of my room. I was really rude to them. I didn't see what those women could do for me; I didn't need their help.

They got up to leave, but, as they opened the door, they told me that they would continue to pray for me. I said they could do whatever they wanted to but I just didn't care, and the ladies left. The last thing I could be concerned about was a bunch of old ladies praying for me.

I found that I had been placed on Tennessee's "Most Wanted" list. They had warrants for me all over. Here I was in the hospital in a cast with my ribs and bones in my shoulder broken. So, the only way I was able to get out and run for it was to take the cast off myself. I cut it off.

I called Sonny, telling him I needed someone to pick me up. Sonny said it was too dangerous because they had an armed guard at my hospital room door.

25

I said for Sonny to be in front of the hospital, and I'd be out. Sonny sent a taxi, and I moved into action.

I slid around the corner away from the armed guard in front of my door. The doctors had said that I couldn't walk, so they were watching for someone in a wheelchair. I made my way out the front door of that hospital in excruciating pain, got into the taxi, and rode away. I felt that I had foiled them again.

I got to Sonny's, and he was no help—I was too hot to handle. There was no place to stay, so there had to be some fast thinking.

Sonny called a man by the name of Frank who previously had been assigned to kill me. He didn't kill me, and he became my friend after the organization realized that I wouldn't rat on them. (More on this later.) So, Frank picked me up and took me to his hideout in Chattanooga.

We left Frank's house to collect on some money that was owed us, and Frank had a wreck. It threw me out on that same side where my ribs were crushed from the wreck not a week before. Frank just walked away and left me there.

It began to pound into my head that Frank was hoping I would get caught. Realization set in—these people didn't care about anyone but themselves. I got up and managed to get back to Frank's house in such tremendous pain that it was all I could do to put one foot past the other.

The only way I was able to stand all that pain was because of all the alcohol in my system. I was staying pretty-well drunk. My pain was severe, and here I was struggling alone, yet still alive.

When I got back to Frank's house, another man had showed up, and they were trying to figure out what to do. Since "the big guy" in the organization had sold everyone down the river, they had to figure out what their plan of action was going to be.

The TBI[1] was rounding up all the members of the organization they could find. One by one each one would fall.

Frank's brother-in-law took the rap for him. The brother-in-law wanted Frank to stay home with his sister (Frank's wife) and take care of her. There was honor among thieves, and Frank's brother-in-law didn't want his sister to be hurt by this and left alone. Blood was thicker than water, and Frank's brother-in-law had great concern for his sister. So, Frank was spared from this roundup that was sweeping through the organization. Frank had slipped through their fingers. He had defied the authorities and somehow managed to avoid being sent away one more time.

---

[1] Tennessee Bureau of Investigation

Chapter 8

Face to Face With Death
(Again)

Many little incidents had happened *before* the time that Frank and I had our encounter in Manchester. I had managed to avoid our imminent confrontation up until then.

The organization had told me that I needed to be a front man or else I would no longer have the luxuries I was accustomed to. I had to make a choice. They had me in a place where I didn't want to lose everything I had been working for all this time for my wife and myself.

I decided that I would do whatever they told me to do. I started being the lead man. One of the big men out of Chattanooga and Atlanta liked to have back-up with him when he went into the bars in Chattanooga. He wanted a man with a gun to go in front of him, and, if he told you to, you would have to shoot someone. That was my job description.

I was the one chosen to take that position, or I would lose everything I had. I knew this man, had been to his house, met his wife, and had met all the people in this organization. I knew the people I was dealing with.

The day came when I did have to shoot a man, although he did not die. (He later died of alcohol poisoning.) The police came and got me and put me in jail. Well, I was waiting for the men in the organization to come and get me out. No one came from the organization; my mother got me out. I could not go back to White County, so I went to my mother's home.

My wife and I had two children by that time. She came from White County to stay with me at my mother's house in Crossville. (Crossville is in Cumberland County, next to White County.) For some reason, Connie had to go see her grandmother. There may have been illness in the family—I can't recall exactly, but she had to leave.

They sent a man named Frank Downey to kill me. (This is the same Frank I mentioned earlier, although this incident happened before that one. Frank is now serving time in prison for killing a police officer. Frank can verify this story.[2]) He was paid to kill me, but I was always a step or two ahead of him.[3]

Being the alcoholic that I was, that day I had walked to the store to get a six-pack of beer. When I returned to my mother's house, a man was sitting at the kitchen table. He had a sawed-off twelve-gauge shotgun resting on the table. It was Frank, my executioner.

This somber man with the shotgun asked if my name was Ralph, and I said, "Yes, it is."

He said, "I've come to kill you. I have a death warrant for you, and I've come to kill you."

He added, "I want to talk to you first. I don't like killing anybody unless I know something about them."

My mother was sitting on the couch, and she was

---

[2] At the time Ralph wrote this, Samuel Frank Downey was in prison for assault with intent to murder; however, Frank died there in 2006, at the age of 78. Frank was converted to Christianity shortly before his death. He always claimed that he was innocent of shooting Walden, TN, police officer Gary Dockery, who later died.
[3] Johnny Ray Graham, the man who sent him, has recently written his own autobiography, "Murders on the Mountain.," which will be published soon.

29

just stunned with disbelief. She couldn't begin to imagine this was happening in her house to her son.

He asked, "What did you do to these men that they're wanting you dead? I'd just like to know."

I was shaking and just about to open a can of beer. I offered one to this man on the other end of the twelve-gauge. He said, with a very somber expression, "Why not."

He watched my every gesture and searched his emotions and my actions for one reason to blow me away.

We sat and drank our beer together. At this particular time, I only weighed about 140 pounds on my 6' 1" frame. I was trembling inside, but I was truthful and straightforward with my appointed executioner. I knew the position I was in, and I could smell the stench of death. It weighed heavy in my nostrils, and I had to play my cards right. This was a game of life or death. What cards did I hold? It was a hand I bet my life on—the truth. I felt as if I were burning up and cold at the same time. Death was close enough that I could feel its cold breath on my neck.

All the things you have heard describing such a position were what I felt. Everything was racing through my head, and my blood seemed to run cold. How close we were in that instant, but I couldn't let him see what I was sensing. I had to think quickly and act quickly with no error. The truth was all I had.

I told him I didn't know why they wanted me dead. I said, "I don't know enough on them to cause them trouble. I've never given them any reason to doubt me."

My uninvited guest said, "The big man feels that you know enough that you need to be killed. That's why they sent me. What do you have to say about that?"

I said, "Well, I don't know. I have no reason to rat on them, and I don't know what they think I know."

We sat there and drank beer a little while longer.

Frank, my special guest, looked at me and said, "I've never killed a young man like you. I don't think I'm going to kill you now. I don't think you're going to do anything to make any trouble. I'm pretty good at reading people when I talk to them. I don't think you are going to tell on them."

As Frank got up to walk out the door, he turned and said to me, "If you call the sheriff on me, I'll come back and kill you."

He gave me no reason to doubt him.

After his ominous form slipped out the door of my mother's house, Mom was hopping mad, and I couldn't blame her. She let me have it. She threatened to run me off because I was always causing trouble. After the shock of it all wore off, she settled down, with far more caution.

Three days before the day this man had come to kill me, the TBI picked up the man who sent Frank on his errand. (Frank didn't know this.) Prior to this, the TBI had scared "the big man" and said that he had to tell them all about the organization, or they would see to it that he would take the whole rap. So they made a deal with him, and he ratted on everybody in the whole system, including me. He remained free for a short time after making this deal, and that's when he devised this plan.

He had sent Frank to kill me, telling the others that I would be the one to tell. He had really intended to use me as his patsy. He was going to wait until I was either killed or picked up before he told the TBI everything he knew; then he would finger me for telling. So, instead of him, they would think that I had exposed them.

They took the big man in and put him in protective custody. No one knows what ever happened to him. (Federal Witness Protection Program?) With his help, they busted the organization wide open. The organization went

31

all the way back into the Sheriff's Department in White County. The sheriff and some of his people were arrested. It was deeply rooted.

At the time, I really never realized how big the operation was.

Sonny never was arrested or questioned about any of this. The bigger organizations have ways to protect their members. So, Sonny never was questioned[4].

Later on, Sonny told me that he had killed seven men. He had been questioned about them, but the police had always turned him loose. They never had enough evidence on Sonny to go to court over any of these deaths.

It turned out that some of the policemen in various towns and counties were involved with the organization. These officers knew what was going on. They knew the ropes.

I finally began to realize that I had let my wife down. I rarely got to see my beautiful green-eyed Connie and our two lovely daughters. I was always going off somewhere to do something to make money to have things I had never had before—yet going nowhere at all. There was always that drive to have more—more than the next guy—more than I'd ever had. I always tried to reach a little bit higher—but I was actually digging the pit a whole lot deeper to set myself up for loss.

In the back of my mind, I still wanted to be able to do something good for my mother. That desire ate away at my insides. I wanted to buy Mother a place of her own for all the hard work she had done for us. All I was doing, however, was bringing more and more disgrace to her, to my wife, to my children, and to myself. I knew I was failing them all.

---

[4] Willard "Sonny" Parks is still alive as of this publication. He is 77 years old.

Chapter 9

The System

It wasn't long before I was back in jail again. This time I got prison time.

They sent me to Cockrill Bend (Riverbend Maximum Security Institution in Nashville). This was the first prison I had been in. It was where a prisoner went through classification.

From there, they sent me to Bledsoe Regional Prison in Pikeville, Tennessee. Bledsoe was near Crossville, and my family would be able to come down to visit me.

Pikeville was a new place. I had graduated up to the "Big Boys." The prison was only a block away from where I had my third experience in a reform school, my path to bigger, not necessarily better, things.

I got to prison and went through my time. I was within a year of being released. I still had charges pending in Crossville for Breaking and Entering, but I thought they had forgotten about them. I thought maybe they had forgotten permanently, lost in the shuffle of paperwork.

Anyway, when I had about a year to go in Pikeville, in 1982, I was put on a work release program in Knoxville.

The officials in the program started allowing me to go out on the streets of Knoxville to look for work. I started selling blood plasma to make money. I started drinking again. As long as I could walk back into the prison, they never said anything to me. So, I never quite got drunk and was able to pull the wool over their eyes. I always drank just enough to keep me going back.

They gave us prisoners two weeks to find ourselves a job. The work release program was based out of the old Eastern State Hospital there in Knoxville. The prison charged you fifty cents for a ride to town to look for a job. If you were on a work release program, you had to pay for your prison meals and room while you were there. If you didn't have a job, you had to go back to the main prison. But, if you were making an earnest effort to find work, they would give you thirty days to look.

Finally, I found a job. I was still in prison, but I now had a job at a furniture company.

The prison always took our paychecks, but my boss paid me some cash besides my payroll check. The officials would always keep books to track what the prisoners made. We could get a $50 draw out of it if we needed it.

The prisoners on work release would work jobs where people would compensate them twice—once for the record and once under the table. We always worked deals with our employers, and the employers were very cooperative.

On the job I was working on, we were constructing a building. When we finished it, the employer didn't need us anymore. I was worried about what I was going to do for work. A man told me he would be able to get me a job working at the World's Fair, which was held in Knoxville in 1982.

He did just that. I got the job at the World's Fair, working in the Pierre Interlude Restaurant as a busboy.

Little did I know that the busboy got to pick up the wine carafes after customers finished eating. The carafes

34

were never quite empty. No one drank directly out of them; they were only poured from. So another busboy and I had about a gallon of wine every day. We would come back so drunk we could hardly walk, and we never did without our wine.

Another thing, every two weeks, the busboys would get ten percent of all the waiters' tips. Besides our regular paycheck, we would get $150 to $200 in tip money.

Just before I left the World's Fair, I got a job in a bar at the Market Square Mall in Knoxville.

There was a Turkish man who wanted to help me. He had bought a building on Market Square Mall. He told me, "You run the bar. As long as you make money, we'll stay open."

I agreed to do it. I forged papers saying I was working in a shop that the owner of the bar had away from the bar. But, instead of working there, I was really working in the bar. If they had known I was working in a bar, they would have sent me back to prison to stay.

So now, here I am in prison, and I'd get the 6 a.m. bus out. I'd never eat breakfast at the prison; I would go right to the Market Square Mall and open up the bar. It had games and pool tables. I'd sell beer all day long—and I'd drink beer all day long. Then at 10 o'clock at night I would close the bar and give this Turkish man, Frank, the money. He'd count the money and write a check to give to the prison officials to keep them happy.

One day the other inmates found out where I was. The way it happened was this: They would have checks from selling their plasma, so they would come in to drink. One of the guys asked me to give him credit. I gave him a couple of dollars of credit. The next day, the same guy came in. He had spent his check somewhere else, but still

35

wanted credit from me. I wouldn't give him anymore credit. So, he told on me.

It was St. Patrick's Day. We had green beer, and we were just having a big old party when a mall police officer came in. A sergeant of the guard, two other guards and a counselor came in from the prison. The counselor walked over, looked around at all the people and then looked at me: "We want to talk to you tonight as soon as you get in." Then, he just turned and they all walked out.

My heart sank—right then, I knew that I was in a heap of trouble. That night, when I walked in the door of the prison, everybody was sitting there waiting for me. They were as afraid as I was.

They said, "We are afraid you are going to let the papers get wind of what you are doing, and you're going to close us down. We'll work a deal out with you. We're not going to say anything to you, and you don't say anything to the media about what you've been doing since you've been here. Tomorrow morning you're going to find another job. You're not going back to that job."

So, I agreed.

I went back to the job, but I hired a girl off the street to work the bar. I stayed in the background to see who was coming and going. I could walk through another business nearby if someone came in that I didn't want to see me. I covered my tracks well.

This worked all the way up until the time I was told that I had to go to court. I thought I'd be going home; I had served my three-to-five years that they had given me. One week before time to go home, the old Crossville charge of Breaking and Entering came back up. It was not going to go away either—it had come back to haunt me.

I was told that I should have never been brought up

on work release, so they sent me back to Crossville on the old charge! It hit me real hard.

Chapter 10

Time Runs Out

Well, there I was—I had just finished work release, and now I was facing more time. They sent me back to Crossville to jail.

The District Attorney in Crossville told me that there was no way I could serve three-to-five years running concurrently with my old sentence. She said I was going to do that three-to-five years.

I had just gotten through doing a whole five-year sentence. I was supposed to get out within thirty days. Now I would have to start all over. I was about to face my past.

My mind just exploded. I went ahead and pleaded guilty to it. I knew that I was guilty, and that I was going on back to prison.

After pleading guilty, I just packed my stuff up and escaped. I wasn't going to stay there any longer. I couldn't stand the thought of staying there five more years.

My wife and kids thought I was coming home. So when I escaped, I went home, and the very first thing I did was get drunk again. I'd been drunk the last two years of my life in prison.

I went to my wife's house first, and she pretty well told me that she didn't want me there, and that I was nothing but trouble. We had three children by then. She said that my two oldest children were afraid of me.

My heart sank.

So we talked for a long time, and I started to lay down. But before I could lay down, the deputies and sheriff surrounded the trailer. I got out of the trailer, and I outran the deputies. They couldn't find me because it was dark, and I was out in the woods.

I ran and got over the mountains to my mother's house, and my mother just plainly told me that she didn't want me there. She said that I was just absolutely no good. She said, "You bring trouble to my home every time you come. I don't want you here."

I knew she was right, so I told her, "Okay."

About that time my oldest brother, Billy, came in with a fifth of whiskey. He said, "If you'll sit down and have a drink with me, maybe we can figure out someplace we can take you."

I told him, "I don't know anywhere to go."

Well, Billy and I started drinking, and I passed out. I came to, only to see the sheriff's car pull up.

I was too drunk to do anything. I couldn't move or fight. I had baited my own trap.

The deputy that came in said, "You ain't worth shootin'. You ain't even worth a bullet, but if you try to run again, I'll kill you."

They finally got me and took me into custody. They said, "We hope they keep you where we put you this time. We don't want you back out."

Well, they put me in a maximum security cell in Crossville, in the same place I had been when I was a twelve-year-old truant. It just seemed like a cycle over, over, and over again. It was always right back to the same place. It was like instant replay with the same moves to cause the same responses. I couldn't seem to break it. Why was it that it was always the same? Here I was back at the beginning.

This time, I knew I'd never be able to get out of there. For some reason, something told me that this was it. I felt like I'd been fighting a battle all of my life and was finally whipped. I gave in and said to myself, "Well, this is going to be it."

I had lost my family, my mother, my brothers; I had lost everything. Something kept telling me that I'd never get out of prison again. I knew that I had really hit bottom.

Well, anyway, I was back in jail in Crossville. They had caught me there at my mother's house. It was on a Friday evening. I was on my way to what was the end for me...

Chapter 11

A Crack in a Crusty Heart

Saturday visitation time came and went. No one in my family came to see me.

Usually, someone always came to see me. My younger brother was the jailer there. He didn't even walk up the stairs to see me.

At two o'clock on that Saturday, the Gideons[5] came to give little New Testaments to prisoners and to pray for people.

Brother Earl Reagan (no relation) came, along with Don Crace, to see me. They came in and gave out the Testaments.

Before they left, Earl Reagan asked me if I wanted a Bible. I told him, "I don't want your Bible. I don't want anything to do with you. I want you to leave me alone."

Earl said, "You've got a lot of anger, but the anger's not going to do you any good. You need to let go of your anger."

He shared with me about his being an alcoholic and a drunk. He told me how God had gracefully saved him and helped him to overcome the alcohol addiction.

He left, but before he left, I got a full-sized Gideon

---

[5] An international organization of men (accepted by invitation only) who voluntarily place Bibles in hotel rooms, schools, prisons and other places.

Bible. The Gideons go out to the motels, hospitals, and prisons. If the Bibles get worn, they go in there and take the Bibles and swap them out. They would put new ones in their place.

Earl had an old red-covered Bible with him. He said, "The Lord is impressing me to leave this Bible with you."

I said, "If you want to leave it, just leave it anywhere you want. It don't bother me."

Earl[6] reached through the bars and laid it ever so gently on an old bench next to the steel bunk where I slept. It sat there the rest of the day. Supper came and went.

That night was really cool. Around ten o'clock, the jail was not full of chaos as usual. The lights were out, everybody was asleep. Right outside the jail, at the corner of the building, was a street light. Using that street light, you could get over in the corner of your cell and write a letter or read a book.

That night I got up, and I got to thinking about my life and what all was going on. I remembered all the way back to my youth and all the people that I had abused. My family relationships were in my thoughts, and I began realizing the possibility of never coming out of prison again.

In prison at that time, five and six people a week were getting killed because there were riots and things going on. The prisons were overcrowded with inmates.

I guess, for the first time in my life, I didn't care if I lived or died. I had struggled all my life for survival and had managed to get through, but now I had reached the end

---

[6] Sadly, Earl Reagan is now deceased, but he lived long enough to see my ministry kick off. When his wife died, God permitted me to be the one to preach her funeral.

of my rope. My family was afraid of me; my friends had given up on me and wanted nothing else to do with me; so I now felt as if my life was over. I was at the end of the road with no one to turn to—no one to talk to. That's when I remembered what Earl Reagan said that day about Jesus. That's when I started seeking God to see if he was real.

I started thinking about what Earl Reagan had said: "There is a way you can be cleansed and made whole— God loves you, Ralph."

I sat there and thought about all the things Earl had said to me. I remember saying, "Lord, if you can love me, and if you can forgive me for all that I have done, if you will accept me, just like I am, knowing everywhere I've been and everything I've done, I'll serve you from this day forward and follow you."

I picked up the Bible Earl had left there and read some of the words. I know that night I accepted Christ in that old jail cell. I took that Bible back to bed with me and lay down. I lay there and went to sleep and slept the best sleep I had ever slept. I've heard people say that a burden was lifted, but it was more than a burden; the weight of sin's shackles fell off of me that night.

I witnessed that forgiveness there in the dimly-lit jail cell. God's love broke through and cleaned my heart. For the first time, I was free of the burden of sin. The blackness that had stained my heart was gone. I had readily received God's promises, and God did the rest. God had led two men across my path, two Gideons, at a time that God's Word could pierce my crusty heart—crusted over with sin and rebellion. I had come to the end of all I had known as my life. I knew the jig was up. I knew it, and most of all, God knew it and had it timed just perfectly.

Here was a chance to turn it all around, make it up to my mom and my wife and children. Here in the corner of

43

the jail cell, by the light of a street light, the blood of Christ cleaned me up and stood me on a solid foundation. I knew I would never be the same again.

The next morning, I woke up fresh and was still reading the Bible. Yes, I had been forgiven much, and now all that love flooded my heart. The cleansing of my heart and my soul brought such peace that I could not keep it quiet. I started telling the people in the jail that the Lord had spoken to my heart that night. They all started laughing at me, kidding me. They said, "God don't speak to people that way; you just don't understand."

They called the sheriff and told him that I had gone crazy. They told him I was up there talking about the Lord. They said there was something wrong with Ralph. The sheriff came and checked me out to see if there was something wrong.

The sheriff turned to the others and said, "You'll not have to worry about this boy—where he's going, he'll be there for a long time. I hope that they keep him there forever."

I stayed in jail for about ten days, waiting to be transported to the Tennessee State Penitentiary in Nashville. My brother was the officer who transported me. My own brother took me back to prison. They had ruled to take me to the main prison in Nashville because the "Walls" in Nashville was the only one that would accept me back. They didn't even want me back at the other prisons.

They made special arrangements to take me back to the Walls.

Chapter 12

Defying the Prison Code
(Cheating Death Again)

When I got to "The Walls," they put me under maximum security in a thirty-day lockdown. That's where I would not have any visitors, because I had just escaped. It was closed security. They took everything from me but the Bible.

In thirty days' time, in maximum security, I read nearly the whole Bible. I read all the New Testament and almost all the Old Testament. I couldn't understand the Old Testament, so I started reading the New Testament again. I basically read for thirty days.

God became my closest and best friend there in that solitary state. I was by myself, had no contact except with the guards, and that was minimal. I had a lot of time to think. I was totally alone except for Jesus. His Word became life to me, and I began to grow there in the dark quiet of that prison. I became wrapped up in the love of God.

Then, when I finally did get off closed security, I wanted to go tell somebody what I had done. I went out from behind the "Wall," and the only people I knew there were from my hometown. Ronnie and Charlie Hoover and Leon Meadows, some old friends of mine, all there for murder. Charlie and Ronnie were both my next-door neighbors in prison.

My brother, Lonnie, was over in another unit. He never would come over to see me. He didn't want to have anything to do with me. He had heard that I was reading the Bible, and my own brother wanted no part of me.

My hunger for drinking didn't necessarily leave when I accepted the Lord. In prison, if you've got the money, you can get alcohol. However, I just didn't want to drink. After I got saved in jail, all I could think of was the relationship I had found, and I wanted to find out more about it.

When I got to the prison and got out from behind the Wall, I realized I could get anything I wanted—drugs, alcohol, whatever. You even could buy guns or knives. Behind the prison walls, anything you wanted, you could get. I didn't understand this, but it was possible. My brother carried a .25 automatic the whole time he was there in prison. He knew he'd have to fight to survive.

I never drank while I was in this prison. I had many opportunities to, but I didn't.

I started going to church behind the Walls, and I wanted some way to have access to the whole prison. The only way you could do that was to get a job on the yard crew. James Vandeveer was the Associate Warden. I went to him and asked him if he would give me a job on the yard crew.

He said, "Do you know how many other people want that job too? How long have you been here?"

I said, "I've been here about six weeks."

He said, "Son, there have been people here for five years wanting that job. Why do you think I should give it to you?"

He picked up my record and looked at my name. He said, "Where you from, son?"

I said, "Crossville."

He said, " Is your daddy's name Homer Reagan? I used to run around with your dad when I lived in Crossville. Me and your dad is old drinkin' buddies. What job did you say you wanted?"

I told him, "I want the job working out here on the yard crew."

He said, "It's yours."

He wrote me out a slip and gave it to me. He said, "Take this to Re-class at four in the morning, and the job is yours."

There were five members on the board to reclassify you into whatever area you were to go on. They would look over your record and see what kind of past you had. They re-classed me to go over onto that yard crew.

I got off closed security. Closed security meant all you could do was go eat and go back to your cell. You had very limited contact with anyone on closed security, but I got past that. Now I was on work release, and I sure did feel good.

I went ahead and went to work the next day. That gave me access to the prison chapel and to all the buildings throughout the whole prison. They gave me a little card that gave me access throughout the prison up until nine at night.

James Vandeveer gave me a job that others had wanted for five years, and it made quite a few people mad. He gave it to me as a favor because of having been friends with my dad.

Since I now had access to the whole prison, I started going into cells and preaching the Gospel to people there in prison. They called me a *Bible Toter*. I got spit on. I got cussed. I got called about every name a man could be called in many ways. Here I was, a new man in prison (more ways than one), and I was coming in there telling them about Jesus, and it didn't necessarily work that way with them.

47

Some of them were serving a life sentence. They'd try to get me to shut up, and I would not shut up.

One day there was a riot in Unit 4. In this riot, two men were killed. During the riot, they busted televisions, threw out shaving cream, toothpaste and other personal items.

The night crews went into the cells of the men who caused the riot, cleaning up the busted televisions, shaving cream, toothpaste, and books, and then removed everything except what prisoners were allowed to have under state regulation. They threw the rest out on the walkway. Then the yard crew had to clean that up.

They came and got a young man named Bobby, on the yard crew, to help me clean up the mess off the walkways. While we were cleaning up the mess, the men in the cells told us, "If you touch them things, we'll kill you."

This is when I began to realize what it was to be faithful to God—what I had been reading in the Bible. I never had authority over me or succumbed to it in my life, and the Bible said for me to submit myself to the authorities, because they had to submit to God themselves.

They, the authorities, told me to clean it up, and the guys in the cells told me to leave it alone.

I told the men in the cell, "I would rather obey God."

So I went in and cleaned up, doing what the men in authority told me to do. By submitting to authority, I was doing what God had told me to do. I learned that real quick in my prayer time and Bible studies.

The inmates said, "Well, this is going to get you killed because you're bothering our stuff."

I went ahead and cleaned up anyway. Bobby did too. He was a young black man that I had been ministering

48

to, and I had asked him several times about accepting Christ and living a Christian life.

He said, "Ralph, I just can't do it while I am living here in prison. Maybe I'll be able to do it when I get out; I just can't do it in here."

Two days after the riot and cleaning up the walkways, they grabbed Bobby. Three men stabbed him nineteen times for taking their stuff off the walkways. Well, after they killed Bobby, they sent me word that I was next.

I went down to my cell one night; I don't remember what I was doing. Three men came to my door. They were about the biggest, roughest guys you could imagine, and they were there to put fear in me.

They said, "You know by the laws of the prison that you're a dead man."

I said, "You know, the laws of the Bible say submit to authority. The only thing I was doing was what God had told me to do. God told me to submit to the authority above me, and that's what I done."

They told me, "We know that you're a new man. So, if you'll go to Check-in, we'll leave you alone. If you go back to the yard, you're a dead man."

"Check-in" is a place where you can go if you are afraid for your life. They'll keep you there, bringing food to you and all that.

I told them, "I'll not go to Check-in. I think the Lord is big enough to take care of me."

It was the first time in my life that I had submitted to the authority above me, and I sure didn't think God was going to let me down now.

The trio turned and walked away from me.

A few days later, as I was getting ready to walk up on the yard, four men came. Two went out to either side.

49

One was in front of me and one behind me. I could feel the hair standing up on the back of my neck. These were Muslims.

They looked at me, and one said, "You know what time it is—it's time for you to get what's coming to you."

The only thing I could say was, "To live is Christ, and to die is gain." (Philippians 1:21)

I never will forget his look. He said, "You're serious, aren't you?"

I said, "Yeah, I'm serious."

He said, "Men, leave this guy alone. He's crazy."

They all walked away and left me alone.

From that day on, I was a living testimony in the prison. Here I had a death warrant on me by the Muslims, and they let me live. They had already killed one man. They knew that there was something going on. The inmates saw that the Muslims allowed me to live in spite of a death warrant by prison standards.

Chapter 13

God Speaks

I started going to the prison church services because I wanted to find out more about God and more about what He wanted me to do.

While I was in there, I went to every church service you could think of: Church of Christ, Church of God, Pentecostal. I wanted to find out their theology. I wanted to find out every tidbit I could about what they believed. I was weeding out what the Lord was allowing me to hear. I knew there was something more that I had to learn—lots more.

One night, I was alone in my cell, and God said, "Ralph, I'm going to let you go home."

I just turned and looked around as if I were expecting to see someone there. I said, "Praise God! I'm going home."

Something inside of me began burning. I knew I was going home. I couldn't wait to get back to church. I started telling my Christian brothers. I started telling everybody there that God had told me I was going home.

Most of them said that I was crazy. They said, "God don't talk to you that way. You done the crime, now pay your time, and quit bellyaching."

I said, "I'm not bellyaching; I just know that God

told me I'm going home."

I said, "God's going to let me go home."

Three weeks, more or less, went by, and I began to ask God, "Lord, what's going on? I know I heard You, and I know in the book of Titus, it says that *You* can't lie. What am I doing wrong?"

God spoke to my heart again and said, "Well, it doesn't look like you want to go anywhere."

I immediately just reached over my bed and got a duffle bag out. I filled it with my stuff and set it there next to the head of my bed. I said, "Lord, I'm ready to go."

For the next two days, everybody in prison came by my cell and laughed at the crazy guy who had his stuff packed and ready to go home. They laughed and humiliated me every waking moment of those two days.

Finally, at 7:45 the next morning, they called over the intercom and said, "Reagan, 9439, bag and baggage."

That means you are leaving.

It was shift change. It was like a movie. We were working, and some of the guys just turned and looked at me. These were the guys who said I was crazy when I told them I was going home.

What they didn't know was that God's Word says this: "Therefore, thou son of man, prepare thee stuff for removing, and remove by day in their sight; and thou shalt remove from thy place to another place in their sight: it may be they will consider, though they be a rebellious house." (Ezekiel 12:3)

All I could say was, "I told you so."

They all came running up and started saying, "You are going to go to Knoxville and stay ten days because you've got that felony escape penalty, then you're going to come back. It takes ten days to go there and come back."

I explained that day—there was no way that I would be back behind the walls of this prison except to preach the Gospel of Christ.

They all shrugged their shoulders and laughed at me. They turned and walked away and said, "Nah, we'll see you in ten days."

The guard came out and said, "I get off in fifteen minutes; how long will it take you to pack your stuff?"

I told him, "My things are already packed. You don't have to wait on me."

In the prison, for security reasons, they don't tell you in advance when you are leaving.

The guard didn't believe me until we got to my cell, and he saw that I had all my stuff packed. I got to preach Christ to him all the way back until he got me to the transportation cell. That's where you go in and wait with the other people who are getting out.

It was at this time that I got to witness to a lot of the guards there. These guards told me I was crazy and that I would be back. They all said I was going to Knoxville, and I was just going for ten days and coming back. They said I had to serve out my time over that felony escape.

They all just laughed and went on about it. It was just one big joke to them.

I explained to them that the Lord said I wouldn't be coming back.

It's pretty hard to explain to a prison guard that God told you something. They see a lot of people use religion to get favors or to work their way to prime positions and then do what they've always done. The guards acted as though they had heard it all before.

They came and got me to go to Knoxville. They chained me, shackled me, put a leather girdle around me. They really fixed me up good. They knew that I had a past of escaping. They fixed me up "fit as a fiddle" to transport me to Knoxville, Tennessee, on the felony escape charges.

They didn't know that I wasn't about to try to escape this time. They didn't know that I had a promise to hold on to from my Heavenly Father, and I wasn't going to do anything to blow it.

I gladly donned those shackles and that leather girdle. I was on my way to what God had promised me—I was headed for a miracle.

Chapter 14

Knoxville: Time to Pay the Piper— and Another Miracle

I was transported back to Knoxville and put in a cell.

Don Crace[7], one of the Gideons who had come to see me in Crossville, had been keeping up with me and helping my wife. He and his wife, Janice, had been writing me letters and helping us since they knew that I had received Christ through their ministry of the Gideon Bibles.

Don and his wife came to my court trial.

The court assigned me a Jewish lawyer who was about to transfer to Oklahoma. My case was the last case he had in Knoxville before he was to be transferred to Oklahoma. He had to stay there for my case before he could leave, and he really wanted to get it over with.

He came to me and said that he had already made a deal with the District Attorney to give me two years probation and two years prison on this felony escape if I would plead guilty.

I said, "Well, I'm not going to plead guilty, and I

---

[7] Don Crace died 24 July 2007, at the age of 75, at his home in Franklin, TN, but he had faithfully tried to help me before and after my conversion.

am not going to accept two years. There is a God who told me that I am going home, and I am not to accept any time."

I never will forget that lawyer and his statement. He looked me in the eye, shook his head, and began fussing with his papers. He said, "They always send me the crazy ones. If you don't accept these *two* years, the judge will give you *five* years for this escape."

That conversation was ended. However, while I was waiting a couple of days to go to court, Don Crace went to the authorities and told them that if there was any way possible that I could get out, he had a job waiting for me.

He wanted to help me get out. He was also betting on our Lord Jesus Christ.

Well, the court date came. I entered the courtroom with an air of expectation. I knew that God was going to do something.

Judge Balitsaris, Third District Judge there in Knoxville, Tennessee, called me up and said, "Young man, I have no alternative but to give you the maximum penalty, which is five years, for this felony escape, because you will not make any deals with the state."

My lawyer smirked and said, "I told you that you should have taken the deal that they offered you."

He had already thrown in the towel. He was hurriedly gathering up his things to leave. Oklahoma was a gleam in his eyes.

I bowed my head there in the courtroom and said, "Lord, this is not what you told me."

At that moment, Judge Balitsaris took his glasses off and laid them on the side of his desk. I remember just exactly how he did it. Then, he turned to me and said, "For some unknown reason, something's telling me that I have to let you go. I am giving you a five-year probated sentence for this felony escape. Mr. Reagan, you are a free man."

My lawyer turned to look at me and said, "I didn't have anything to do with that."

I said, "You heard the judge say he didn't have anything to do with it either. Only God can get the glory out of it when it's that way. When you don't have anything to do with it and neither does the judge, that's God. I know what God told me He was going to do, and He did it. That's God."

(Some people may have felt that Ralph Reagan was exaggerating concerning the way things happened regarding this incident, but printed below, verbatim, is the documentation of the State of Tennessee versus Ralph Randall Reagan, alias Escape. It is a matter of record and a testimony of God's miraculous ways.)

Friday, July 6, 1984

Court met pursuant to adjournment, present and presiding, the Honorable George P. Balitsaris, Judge of Division III, Criminal Court for Knox County, Tennessee, when the following proceedings were had and entered of record, to-wit:

THE STATE   No. 18829
VS
RALPH RANDALL REAGAN, ALIAS
ESCAPE

Came the Attorney General for the State, and the defendant with counsel of Record, The Honorable Phillip Vavalides, for entry of judgment. On the 22nd day of June, 1984, the Defendant having pled guilty to the offense of Escape from the Knoxville Community Services Center While Confined therein and Serving a Penitentiary Sentence, as charged, the defendant is convicted of Escape from the Knoxville Community Services Center While Confined therein and Serving a Penitentiary Sentence, as charged. After considering the evidence, the entire record and all factors in T.C.A. Title 40, Chapter 43, all of which are incorporated by reference herein, the Court's findings and rulings are: The sentence imposed is 5 years in the State Penitentiary. It is, therefore, the

58

judgment of the Court that the defendant for the offense for which he stands convicted, to-wit: Escape from the Knoxville Community Services Center While Confined therein and Serving a Penitentiary sentence shall be imprisoned in the State Penitentiary at hard labor for a period of 5 years as a Aggravated Offender, within Range II, and shall pay all the costs of this prosecution; that he be rendered infamous, as provided by law.

Upon recommendation of the Attorney General, this sentence is hereby suspended and defendant is placed on probation for a period of 5 years, probation to expire July 6, 1989. Defendant's probation is conditioned upon his not hereafter violating any of the laws of any City, State of the United States or being guilty of any misconduct inconsistent with good citizenship. The Clerk will furnish a transcript of this judgment to the defendant, his counsel and the state Probation Counselor.

COURT ADJOURNED UNTIL TUESDAY, JULY 10, 1984 AT 9:00 A.M

(S)   GEORGE P. BALITSARIS

GEORGE P. BALITSARIS
JUDGE

59

Chapter 15

Home to a New Life

Well, I walked out of the courthouse that day—almost a *free* man, but certainly a *new* man. I walked out and came back to Crossville.

My wife and our kids had been living in a little one-bedroom trailer. Mr. Crace and his wife had gotten a little old apartment and tried to help us get started. I started working for him at the charcoal plant in Mayland, which is right outside of Crossville. He put me on the yard crew. I started working for him there doing yard maintenance.

We started going to church every time the doors opened. My children had grown, and we were all starting a new life together. Tanya was eight; Sonya, six; and Randall, about four.

I had been in prison about sixteen months. I served about nine months of that sixteen before I got into the work release program. I still had over five years that I should have served for the felony escape, but the judge of the court gave me five years probation instead. Normally, you cannot get probation for the escape penalty. But, after receiving probation for the escape term, I was basically a free man.

One day I was walking down the street. It was raining, and I was walking to work. A deputy sheriff stopped; he thought that I had escaped from prison again.

I told him what had happened, and he said, "No, that's not right, you can't get away with that, you must have escaped."

He called the Central Unit downtown and tried to have me put back in prison. He knew that I was out too soon to have served enough time in prison for escaping.

The probation officer here in Crossville said, "You don't escape and then get put on probation."

The probation officer was not able to get me put back into prison either. Judge Balitsaris had signed my release, pronounced me a free man, and none of them could understand or do anything about it. It is sort of like when Christ pardons our sins; it's once and for all, and it can't be done all over again. That's just like it was with this judge; he signed my release papers, and no one could override them.

It really made this community mad when they couldn't get me put back in prison. The police, the probation officers, and the parole officers did everything they could to get me put back into prison, and they couldn't do it.

Mr. Crace went up and had it out with the probation officers. He said, "This young man has come out and is doing everything he can do. The judge signed his release papers, so why don't you leave him alone."

Don Crace said, "If he falls again, you can have him again. As long as he's not bothering anybody, leave him alone."

They saw that I had people who were going to help me, so they left me alone for a little while. But they always watched me. They wanted me to mess up, so they kept a close eye on everything I did.

The Lord allowed me to crawl out of that darkness and into the marvelous light.

As I write this, all this occurred some seventeen years ago.[8] I thank God for bringing me out, and He has been so good to me. He has really shown me his Hand of Mercy.

Connie, along with our two daughters, Sonya and Tonya, had waited for me to be freed. While I was in prison, we had our little boy, Randall. That was in December, 1979. They're all grown now with families of their own. Connie and I have six grandchildren.

When Randall got big enough to toddle around, he would wear little overalls, carrying a little Gideon New Testament in his front pocket. He said he was going to grow up and be a "pweachuh."

Connie said that those babies were what she got up in the morning for.

Now I look at my son as an adult with a family of his own, and I tell him, "Son, you're everything I wish I could have been at your age." He is a good provider; a good daddy. I guess hindsight is always something we have when we have led a life like mine.

God has truly blessed me, my wife and my kids.

---

[8] Ralph dictated this portion in 2001.

Chapter 16

Backset

I only had a sixth-grade education at the time of my release. I started going to church. I went places giving my testimony, and the Lord started using me. He opened doors for me.

I worked for Hickory Charcoal in Mayland for about five years. But, things started happening; sin entered my life again, and I started drinking again. My brothers died: I lost three brothers within a short time. I couldn't handle it.

For years, a church I had gone to had been promising me that they would send me to college and get me an education. But, they kept on telling me I didn't have enough time behind me; that I wasn't stable enough to proceed with my ministry.

After five years, when all these bad things started happening to me, I fell and went back to drinking. Alcohol had gotten its foot in the door; I had begun drinking again.

My wife ran me off. We really got into it. Everything was falling apart.

I went to Florida for a year. I stayed down there and got a good job. I had promised my boss in Crossville and the people here in town that I would not come back for a year. They were trying to help me stay out of prison.

But, no matter where I went, there was always something drawing me back to this town, Crossville, and to my wife, Connie. After the year was up, I started calling my wife and writing to her. She came down to Florida and stayed with me. We began to work at reconciling our differences.

Connie and I reconciled, and she agreed that I could come back home.

You have to realize something. When there wasn't an ounce of hope, she was still there. When it seemed as though all was lost, after all those years, and after all the tears she had shed over me, she was still hoping for a miracle. She was the woman behind this man.

This is my testimony, but she was always there loving me even when I was not lovable. I put many a tear in my Connie's beautiful green eyes. I heard in a song that tears are a language that only God understands. He heard every tear fall, and He answered every prayer.

If we confess our sins, He is faithful and just
to forgive us our sins, and to cleanse us from
all unrighteousness.

1 John 1:9

Chapter 17

Ministry Begins

After that year in Florida, I came back home to Crossville. My wife and I rededicated our lives to the Lord.

Anything that keeps us from God is sin, no matter how great or small. God had removed and forgiven our sins and restored us to fellowship with Him. When I got back here and rededicated my life to the Lord, I wanted to do everything I could to stay away from alcohol and my old habits.

I felt the church I was attending wasn't giving me the support I needed. I was in a state of need even though I had rededicated my life. I needed encouragement.

I started going to another church, had a good job, and was making good money. Everything started turning upside down again. I don't know if it was a test, a trial or what, but my wife and I stood strong this time. We kept working in the church, working for the Lord. We stayed busy doing what we felt God was calling us to do.

One Sunday at Believer's Fellowship, the church I was attending, I saw a deacon from First Baptist Church, Crossville. He said that he wanted to talk to me. I agreed, and we sat down to discuss some things. I had not spoken to this brother in the Lord for some time and was curious to hear what he had to say.

He got right to the point. He never hesitated, but jumped right in.

"Ralph, I believe you owe it to us at First Baptist to come back and give us another chance. We know we've been mean to you, and we've done some things in the past we are sorry for. We feel that you owe us one more chance."

This was a rather troubling situation, so I talked to my pastor at Believer's Fellowship. Part of me wanted to go, and part of me wanted to stay. The pastor told me that if I felt like I needed to go back, then, I must try it and see how it worked out.

I ventured out to restore the relationship with my former church. They gave me a job. It was a janitor's job, but they also allowed me to start driving the church bus as my ministry.

I would go to all the trailer parks around the city— wherever I could find people to go to church. I would bring three and four van loads of people to church on Sunday mornings.

Folks started getting saved and being baptized— children and adults. One thing led to another, and it got to where there were so many people from the trailer parks coming that the church couldn't hold them.

It's sad to say, but one of the deacons came to me and said, "We don't want these people here." He said, "They are not *our kind* of people, not from our social walk, and they don't belong here at our church."

I looked at him in astonishment and asked, "What do you want me to do with them? They're people that need to hear the gospel!"

They made a deal with me that if I would go back to school and get my education, they would help me find a

66

place to take "these people."

I had left that church the first time because they had made that same promise to me, and they didn't keep their word. Here we were again; it had come full circle. Now they wanted me to go to school and prepare for another letdown!

The Lord had worked it out where they were pushing me to go to school, and it had worked out in God's time. God knew the time, and He put the pieces in place for His plan to be carried out. It all fit into His blueprint to strengthen me and for them to see how dedicated I was to fulfilling the vision and call that God had put on my heart to do.

Chapter 18

Fulfilling the Vision

I got ready to go to school. We found a college in Kentucky that would accept me with only a sixth-grade education. They put me on remedial status. I went to high school at night and college during the day. At the end of the first year, I was taking 16 college credits. I was driven by the promises I knew in my heart that God had given me.

In December of my first year at college, I passed my GED[9]. The following semester, I was put under college accreditation. I was officially in a college class. I went straight through college.

I would drive back and forth to Tennessee, and I would only see my wife for a day and a half per week. Friday, I would come in from Kentucky. Saturday, I would go to the trailer parks and get the people prepared to go to church on Sunday. I would visit them and let them know that I would be there at a certain time to pick them up. I'd pick them up on Sunday, take them home after church, and then leave to go back to school in Kentucky.

---

[9] GED stands for General Educational Development. GED tests are a battery of five tests developed by the American Council on Education (ACE). When passed, ACE certifies that the taker has high-school-level academic skills. These tests were originally created to help veterans after World War II.

My wife loved me, and sometimes she may not have understood my drive, but she knew I wasn't drinking anymore. She knew that I was serving the Lord. She knew I wasn't living a life of shame, and I wasn't in prison. She supported me in prayer, and she was there for me even if it was just one-and-a-half days a week.

I did this for three-and-a-half years. A lot of people were being saved and baptized. A lot of them went to other churches.

I graduated with a good grade point average (GPA). I graduated with one of the highest honors given by the college, the Evangelism Discipleship Award. This award recognizes those who exemplify a balanced approach in sharing the gospel and discipling new converts.

Presently, I am working on my master's degree in Biblical Theology. I expect to graduate in October 2008.[10]

Originally, I was working towards a master's degree in Apologetics. An Apologist defends the *faith*, not defending *God*, by showing the truth out of scripture to those being led away by cults.

That is the working of the mission field. We work with everyone from every background and different people who come from all types of beliefs.

The Bible says that we need to have an answer for every person who asks. The Apologist tries to express the hope of Christ and give the answer that is needed for any religious system.

I switched to Biblical Theology because I felt it would give me a better foundation and knowledge of the Bible. I can still follow the principles involved with the Apologetics, but Biblical Theology will give me a much broader scope of knowledge.

---

[10] Ralph actually completed his Master's Degree in Biblical Theology in March 2008.

Biblical Theology studies the Bible from the perspective of understanding the *progressive history* of God revealing Himself to humanity following the Fall and throughout the Old Testament and New Testament. It particularly focuses on the events of the Old Testament in order to understand how each thing ultimately points forward to fulfillment in the life mission of Jesus Christ.

When I came back from school, we continued to go to First Baptist Church in Crossville. That's where I was bringing all the people referred to earlier. The church welcomed me back and gave me a position as Assistant Pastor.

All this happened, but I still had the call to this ministry that we have now established here. That's when our pastor charged the church's Board of Directors to get the Bread of Life Rescue Mission established.

We started through the First Baptist Church, got our 501(c)(3) non-profit status, a pro bono lawyer, Randall York, and the church support.

We started into the process of opening the mission January of 2001. We now serve more than 3500 meals a month, thirty to forty persons per serving. We sleep anywhere from sixteen to thirty people each night.[11]

(On special occasions, such as Christmas and Thanksgiving, volunteers from various churches in the county bring an abundance of food—an enormous amount of food—to the mission. They bring huge pans of ham, turkey, dressing, gravy, cranberry sauce, sweet potatoes, mashed potatoes, corn, green beans, peas, deviled eggs, and so forth. Many of them stay to eat with us. We always invite anyone who needs a good meal to come for these

---

[11] The mission now serves around forty persons per meal. They have between thirty-five and forty persons staying overnight every night.

dinners.)

We are starting to see fruit spring forth. We see people going through transition from being dependent on this mission to having their own home.

So, we have people coming off the streets, getting jobs and taking the money they have saved for thirty days to rent their own home or apartment. They don't have to go ask for help from the churches or community.

The response to this from the people is great. We have several families that are in this transition even as we speak. The churches and the community are taking notice of what is happening with the people we are ministering to.

My wife does most of the cooking. She helps to teach and guide the other women in the Lord, in everyday growth and in personal care, as needed.

We were staying here and going home rarely. Since we began this book about my life, Connie and I have lost our home but are in full charge of operating the mission now. We are here day and night. We feel the responsibility of the vision that God has given, and this is where he wants us.[12]

We don't want anyone to abuse this opportunity or this home that God has provided for many. We don't want it to acquire a bad name as poor stewards of God's possessions.

We are keepers of the vessels, a lot like Samuel was as a small boy. He kept the vessels in the temple. We keep the earthen vessels who are new Christians or are seasoned Christians who have fallen on hard times.

We don't want people to think this is a flophouse or a place for drunks. It's not—it is God's house. We want

---

[12] Since that writing, Ralph and Connie have obtained a home and have been able to hire staff to oversee things at night.

people to recognize this as a place where God changes people's lives. This is Holy Ground. It is a place to sustain those in need. The Bread of Life is a conduit for hope.

We feel that we are meeting all the requirements. We have potential for expanding by buying the building across the street, and, because of the needs, eventually next door, as well.[13]

I can hardly wait to see what God is going to do in this place. God only knows! I wake up every morning with an anticipation of the day ahead and what God is going to do, before I ever put my feet on the floor.

My mother is alive[14]. She is seventy-nine years old and in good health. She works in the garden. She got saved a few years back.

My wife, my mom, my children are all saved. We have had tremendous revival in my family.

Of course, there are trials that come, but God promised me He would carry me through them. Just as He promised to take me home from prison, He has seen me through each day. He has shown me more than I ever expected and has taken me farther than I could have conceived.

He took me to the mission field in Russia for twenty-eight days, Haiti for five weeks, and I have been invited to go to Cuba[15]. I have spoken to many people throughout the world, including several states in the United States.

People ask me why I want to go where other people don't want to think about going. My response is that where people don't want to go is where God wants us to go. I

---

[13] Construction began on the new facility in 2010. The building referred to above was demolished to make room for the new facility.

[14] In 2004, Ralph's mother passed away.

[15] He did go to Cuba.

want to go where God wants me to go, not for a luxurious vacation or pleasure trip, but for the souls of men.

God longs for fellowship with mankind, for He created us to fellowship with Him. He wants us to be with Him at the end of our lives. He wants each of us to know His great love and to trust Him to get us through our daily problems. God wants us to trust Christ as our Savior. He wants us to meet Christ as our Savior so that we may understand the very center of John 3:16

For God so loved the world that He gave His only begotten son, that whosoever believeth in Him should not perish, but have everlasting life.

God sent Connie and me to this mission. If the churches of America could just see, the lost don't want to go to church. In most cases, the church has nothing to offer the lost. It is sad to say that many times it does not meet their need.

Don't get me wrong—people are being saved, but those outside the church building need the Lord. I reached many people with the bus ministry that otherwise would not have stepped through the church doors.

Those who are lost and have been on the streets have a degree of discernment regarding churches because they have not had the love of Christ shown to them by members of those churches. If a ministry is not truly a God-given ministry, those who have walked out in the world will know.

If the lost just get a taste of the true love of Christ, they will respond. They will either run *to* it, or they will run *from* it. There are those who drink God's love up as if they were sponges. I did.

If they are as willing to give God's love as they themselves have received it, those are the ones that God can use.

Chapter 19

The Mission Medical Clinic
Background and 2010 Update

I went out to Fairfield Glade, and I spoke to a church, telling them the vision that God had given me to start this place. After speaking, I always ask if anyone has any questions. One guy stepped up and said, "I heard you talk about giving food to people and giving them a place to live; you give them clothing—but what do you do about medical?

I told him, "Well, I'm not a doctor."

And he said, "Well, I am. I'm going to come over to give you assistance."

He came over a couple of days later—Dr. Keith Brown—and we started talking. Shortly after that, I had an opportunity to go to Nashville where they were closing down one of the old missions there on Seventh Avenue, and they told me I could have anything I wanted from that old mission for this mission. So, I rented a truck, and I went down, and I got all the stuff out of the doctor's office— tables, chairs, and all the different things. I brought them here, and we set up a little medical clinic, and on Mondays and Thursday nights we started seeing patients.

And, it started growing. We had some people from Fairfield Glade First Baptist come to set up the records. When it first started, it was real small; we were seeing five or six patients a night, and it grew and it kept growing.

One night, one of the volunteer doctors, Dr. David Litchford, asked, "Do we really need this place here?" And, I said, "Dr. Litchford, all we ask is for doctors to give two hours once a month to see someone who may need some help."

He said, "I don't really think we need this."

Well, the first patient that God sent to him was a man who had got thrown from a horse. He could hardly walk. He was using a walking stick, and he was shaking. Dr. Litchford looked at this man and sent him straight to the Emergency Room, where he got a doctor to do the surgery on him. The man had something seriously wrong in his back. If he hadn't been here to see that man and diagnose him, Dr. Litchford said the man would have been paralyzed for life if he'd been like that another day or two. So, the man was that close to being paralyzed for life. Because of this place being open, that man is alive and can still walk. He comes by and thanks us from time to time for what we do here.

God really wanted to show Dr. Litchford what we do here at this place, so he sent him another patient who had melanoma cancer—the man had a little brown spot on his chest. Dr. Litchford sent him to the hospital. If he hadn't caught it then, in the early stages, the man would have died.

The third time Dr. Litchford came, God sent him another patient. This patient's blood sugar was up to 900! Dr. Litchford sent him for care. That was three lives that God placed in front of Dr. Litchford to show him how needed this little place was for people who didn't have insurance. God got his attention, and now Dr. Litchford never misses. He says he has it on his computer calendar, so he won't miss it. He doesn't want to miss that time because he knows how it's needed.

A lot of people won't go see a doctor because they're afraid of doctors or are embarrassed because they don't have money, but they will come here because we have a policy that you don't have to have the money; you don't have to have insurance. So they'll come in to see the doctor with a little bit of ease. We've found a lot of people here who are really, really needful for medical reasons. And, it all started because Keith Brown heard the need, and God's people rose up when they realized that's what they were here to do.

We now have several doctors working in the clinic. Where the medical clinic is now used to be my office; Keith put me out of my office and put me on the road.

God said, "The poor you will always have with you." We as a Christian nation need to understand that God has given us one of the greatest responsibilities in the world. When we become a Christian, we don't become a Christian to go to church, sit on a pew, listen to the preacher, then go home and think about what he says until the next week. We're supposed to utilize the gifts and talents that God has given us in the work of the kingdom somewhere. We're supposed to come back to the church and let the church know what's going on with our gifts and talents. The pastor can feed us and encourage us to go out and do more. That is the real proof of a true church.

Keith Brown and I went to the hospital (Cumberland Medical Center) together and talked with Jim McMackin, who was head of the hospital at that time. Mr. McMackin just happened to be a Gideon, and he'd read my testimony, so he knew where I was coming from and what I'd been doing.

He said, "We want to help any way we can." So, the next time the doctors had their annual meeting, Mr. McMackin told them what was going on here, and that got

77

some other doctors involved. Then, those doctors told other doctors, and that's how we got to fourteen.

After Mr. McMackin retired, Ed Anderson took over, and I went over and talked with him a couple of times, and he's increased the borders there in the hospital to the place where he wants to help us with some other different specialties. He's got a new orthopedic surgeon there, and he'd like to get him involved with our mission helping the indigent people with that type surgery.

So we also have the hospital involved to where he brings lunch every Wednesday for the people here. And, the staff at the hospital comes over to serve. That includes the doctors, nurses, the cleaning people, the maintenance men, everybody. They sign up on a sheet of paper posted over there, and they come over and serve the food on Wednesdays.

We now average anywhere between 50 and 75 patients per month. If you take 50-75 patients per month away from the Emergency Room, and you multiply that to the yearly number (600-900), then you can see how much money that saves the hospital and taxpayers. The doctors donate their service, but sometimes patients have to have x-rays and lab tests made...

Mr. McMackin was not showing enough usage of federal funds by the hospital and was actually praying on an airplane coming back from a meeting to find a way to see more people and use more federal funds to keep from losing that status. And that's when Dr. Brown and I went in to talk with him—it was the right time—it dovetailed together. He had just got back from that meeting. We were praying before we left here that God would open his heart up to give us a bit of the indigent care there, and Mr. McMackin was looking for someone they could help, so it really worked out great for the hospital and for us because

78

now we get the federal status for our patients here. Now, if indigent people need blood work or x-rays, they can get it free. The hospital charges us for it, but they charge it off on the federal at the end of the year.

But, if someone needs surgery or an EKG or something of that magnitude, we have to let them see the second person in charge at the hospital. Usually they work it out to where they can do it even though it is so expensive. If we sent too many for that type thing, they wouldn't be able to afford it, but we've been blessed, and we have a good rapport.

The Medical Clinic is free to those who cannot pay, but those who can pay are asked to do so. Those who can pay are charged small fees according to their ability to pay. We use a system based on their family income and the number in the family.

Someone has asked, "Why are these people not on TennCare?" Well, the answer is that the state of Tennessee has insufficient funds to provide medical care for all who actually need it. Thousands have had to be dropped from TennCare coverage, leaving them with no means for receiving medical care. (TennCare is a government-operated medical assistance program designed for people who are eligible for Medicaid, as well as for some children who do not have insurance. TennCare is a Medicaid waiver, or demonstration, program. Its purpose is to demonstrate that the use of managed-care principles can generate sufficient savings to enable the state to cover more than Medicaid-eligible people.)

The clinic medical volunteers include internists, a gynecologist, an ophthalmologist, and several in family practice. In addition, when a specialist of a particular type is needed, they have but to call their colleagues, who always respond to the need.

Some of the doctors presently volunteering at the clinic are Doctors: Stacey Carlton, Stephen Clark, Thomas Clayton, James Johnson, Mark Lee, David Litchford, Kimberly Peaslee, Dale Perrigan, Mark Hendrixson and John Sherrill. Others who have volunteered in the past were Doctors Buchanan, Lewis, Lively. Pitt and Wilson. This list is not all inclusive, nor does it include the names of the doctors' colleagues who perform services upon request.

There is a great need for a volunteer dentist. We have many people coming in with abscessed teeth and other painful dental conditions. They are in horrible pain, and we can only send one dental patient per month for treatment.

Many nurses come regularly for two-hour sessions to provide such services as blood pressure and vital signs checks, to assist the doctors, and to help with paperwork. These doctors and nurses come to the mission to volunteer after having put in full shifts at their regular practices or the hospital; sometimes beginning as early as 6:00 a.m. Some of the doctors even return to their own offices after the clinic closes so they can finish their own work.

The Nurse Coordinator is Rebecca Foster, and some of the volunteer nurses are Sharon Barrett, April Collins. Bertha England, Harriett Engstrom, Lydia Horner, Marti Maxwell, Becky McKinney, Maureen Noel, Regina Randolph, Joan Robbins, Keith Robbins, Deb Sapp, Beverly Schwind, Karlene Sullivan and Sheila Sutton. Some of the former nurse volunteers were Jeannie Lynn and Hope Francis. Hopefully, we haven't left anyone out.

Volunteers such as Lois Ragsdale (the Coordinator), Linda Connelly, Mary Greene, Frances Anne Gwin, Vernita Haig, Linda Hassler, Nancy Ott, Milda Pierce, Karin Riffe, Twila Stidham, and many others help with reception and paperwork in the Medical Clinic. Among those who were the early visionaries but who are no longer in the vicinity or able to help were: Karen Brown (wife of Dr. Keith Brown), Carla Lockard, Bettye Lunn, and Helen O'Dell. (This list may not contain everyone who has ever assisted with this work.)

Chapter 20

Miracles on Fourth Street
(From an interview with Ralph in 2010)

From the day that we opened, me and Rupert Maxwell prayed that God would give us what we need to take care of this place. Both buildings were empty; we didn't have *anything* in them. We started praying, and in less than five weeks, we had everything we needed in these buildings. I made a specific prayer that we needed so many beds, and in less than two weeks, I got a call from Sparta telling me that the nursing home was going to change out beds, so I went down and got the beds.

I didn't have help bringing the beds into the building, and I hurt myself so bad that I was in Intensive Care and almost died. They gave me a blood transfusion because I busted myself open. And then the doctor told me I couldn't go back to work for so many days, but God miraculously healed me so that in less than ten days, I was back out doing what I needed to do.

When we first opened, I was doing six nights a week here at the Chapel, plus one night a week at the jail service, plus I was doing Sunday morning services here. In that time, we were so busy, time got away from us; we didn't know where it was going so fast. Then, I began speaking for the Gideons; going out of town and even out of the country.

The first year, God gave me another vision in my heart that I needed more property than I had. So, I went to the bank, and every time something would come open here adjoining our property on Fourth Street, I would buy it. I used my personal credit to go to the bank to buy it, then I would re-sell it penny-for-penny to the Mission. So, I bought up these two blocks here by doing that.

Even though I was on the hook for the loan, I knew it would be taken care of. One thing I've come to find out in this ministry, God may not give you everything you want, but He'll give you everything you need. He's always provided it. For instance, one Thanksgiving we had a lot of people from Fairfield Glade and other places volunteering, and my wife needed some brown sugar, and she didn't have any. We stopped and prayed. We said, "Lord, you know what we need—we need brown sugar." It was Thanksgiving Day. Less than ten minutes later, a man called us and said, "I've got some brown sugar. Would you all like it?" We didn't know how much he had, and he brought us five 50-lb bags of brown sugar!![16]

Anyway, whenever we pray, we pray specifically for whatever we need, and God's always provided for us. Sometimes more, and sometimes less. It's always enough to get us through.

We've never, since we've been open, had to go borrow money—yet. And we pray that God will keep blessing us so that we can just keep going. The main objective of this whole program is to get God's Word to people who usually will not go to a church service anywhere.

---

[16] In case you're wondering what on earth they did with 250 pounds of brown sugar, they took the excess, placed about two pounds each in baggies, and put it into their food boxes.

83

For instance, they may feel their clothes are not good enough. That's the reason I never wear a tie here; I always wear my Levis. You know, in the story of Christ, anywhere and everywhere Christ was, He always came down to the level of the person he was speaking to. He never tried to supersede them, never tried to show His authority; He never tried to show anything of that nature. He always tried to be humble; He tried to be meek with them and straight to the point.

I feel that's what God has given me more than anything—he's given me a good discernment of the spirits to where I can tell if a person is truthful with me or not, and I believe that God has given me a good discernment of it, and He blesses me more than I ever deserve. I know that the blessings He gives us are not for us, but are for other people.

I tell people I'm more the middle man in the Kingdom's work. If you think about it, how many people give us the couches, chairs, beds, clothing, shoes, and stuff because they don't really know where to take that merchandise to make sure that it gets to people who need it. I have an open door policy here—people know that they can some here and get those things if I've got them. So, I give the blessings that other people give to us to other people who really need them; so we're all being blessed. But while the person's here, they hear the Gospel, so according to Philippians, whenever someone is saved, the fruit of that is returned back to the person who gave to us in the first place, and we all get rewarded when we get home. So, I am the middle man, and it's a blessing to be the middle man.

You see, growing up, I never thought in a million years I'd be back here within one block of the housing project where I grew up. Here, I'm in a place and a position to help people. In my lifetime, even when I didn't know the Lord, I always felt bad for other people and had pity on them because they didn't have things. It really hurt me, and I had a deep concern, and it really hurt me because I couldn't give to them.

I remember back whenever I was thirteen or fourteen years old, whenever I asked Christ into my life the first time. I don't know if I really meant it then or not. I didn't really know what I was doing. I just prayed that one day I would have enough that I could give to other people. So, God's honored that prayer because He knew that whenever I prayed that prayer, I prayed it sincerely. The things I get, I don't really want them for myself, I want them so that I can bless other people who need them—me and my wife both feel that way.

For eighteen months, when we first opened the Mission, my wife never got paid a dime, but she was here working twenty-four hours a day, seven days a week. We never had a vacation; never had any time off. Sometimes we'd get a day here or a day there. She never complained; never told me that it was too much; even today, even with her physical condition as it is, she still does as much or more than I do.

I feel that God has now given us enough property to take care of the vision we have to take care of the indigent people, the people who are homeless, and we're going to transition the women and children from here straight into a home. We do more of that than we do anything.

The new place will house one hundred people— fifty beds for women and children, and fifty beds on the other side for men. The dining area will be in the middle— separating the two—out of the dorm right into the dining room. It's going to be really nice facility for people to come to, and it's also going to be used as an emergency shelter

85

for the American Red Cross for any other tragedies that cause them to need to put people somewhere for a few days. It's not just for transitional housing for the homeless men, women and children, but it's also a place of refuge for people in case of major tragedy.

People will be able to stay until they can do better. What we're going to do is, once we get this built over here, we want to utilize this old part for what we call the second phase. The second phase will be for people who need a little more time.

We're going to start a house program downstairs where we'll have five or six men with a section for each one of them. They'll be on a six-month basis. They'll still have to abide by all the rules, attend chapel, etc. During that six-months period, what we want to do is help get them a job and get them into a banking system to show them how to take care of their finances; how to shop at the grocery store for cheaper items; help them learn to budget.

These are some of the issues that a lot of people have; they don't know how do things to take care of their money. Ninety percent of the people who come through here don't have a high school diploma. What we want to do is make sure that if they want school, we help them. We've helped seven students go through college. We help people to get their GED. We have a GED program, and we have a program to help adults learn to read. Anything in the educational area that people want help with, we'll help them to get into that program. They've got to utilize their efforts too. If they get into a program and don't show any initiative in it, if they don't put any effort into it... For instance, we've had some guys we placed into a school program, and they didn't like going back to school; they thought it was silly—they were just doing it to have a place to stay. We want people that will really be interested in it because it takes a lot of financial assets and a lot of time to do it. It takes a lot on both sides, and if you waste a person's time, a mentor or tutor, for weeks, and then just drop out, that's their time and our time that's been wasted. It's really hard to know if a person is going to follow through with it; you've got to have a lot of discernment to know if they really want the help.

We sent one of the gentlemen now working in the jail ministry with me through college for five years.

He made a statement to one of his friends, "Mr. Reagan is here to help me, and I see my way out. I don't need to go to jail, because he's going to get me out. I'm going to play the game." Well, he came out to play the game, but once he got out, and he came here and started hearing the Word of God preached to him, he was convicted, saved and baptized.

Then he went to college and stayed for five years, and now he's come back, and he tells people, "You can't play with God." His name is Kirk He married a girl, and she went to college with him, and he's out of college now. He's taken over the jail ministry for more than a year now. He also works with us here at the mission.

God says in Isaiah 55:11, "My word will not return unto me void, but will accomplish whatever I set it forth to do, and it will prosper." I don't remember it verbatim, but I know the first part says, "My word will not return unto me void."

I've watched a lot of men—this is where people say to me, "Ralph, why do you give your time and effort to these men in the jail and on the streets when all they're doing is playing the game?" Well, I say this, "The rich man, the poor man, the middle man, they all have to come to Christ the same way; there's none that can go to Him differently." God calls everyone the same way. Romans,

Chapter 10, says, "How shall they know if someone doesn't tell them?" So, we've got to tell them; then it's up to the Holy Spirit to convict them and do the rest. One sows and one waters, but it is God who gives the increase.

We had a gentleman come in, and I hadn't talked with him in over two years when he came to my office, sat down and started crying. A big, young man with a family. He said, "Mr. Reagan, I want to tell you something. We used you. We came in here and got money for this and that, and I was taking my money and buying drugs. But I knew there was something different. Every time I would do it, I felt bad. I didn't think I even had a conscience, but I knew something was different, and one night I woke up, and I got on my knees and said, 'God, if this is what it feels like to be drawn by the Holy Spirit, I want to give it up right now to you. I'm sorry for what I've done, and I want to accept Christ as my Savior, and I promise you I'll never steal another dime of your money.'"

He came back in to share that with me, and while we were sitting there talking, I prayed with him. He went to Ohio, and got back into church in Ohio. The pastor of that church in Ohio called me about six months later and told me that the young man's family was there and still in the church and that the young man was doing great. He said the young man was a great Bible student, and that he was just bubbling over with the spirit of God in his life. So, we never know what we're doing in the lives of other people.

One deacon from a church here in Crossville came to me one day and said, "Did you give that boy some money here?" I said, "Yes, I did." He said, "Do you see how big he is? I don't want you giving him *my* money that I give to *you*."

I said, "Wait a minute, let me tell you about that man that just walked out of my office. Number one, he's been a truck driver for over eighteen years. He was told three years ago that his upper and lower back had to have surgery. So they went in and they removed so many discs out of his back, and they told him he would never be able to drive again. He didn't have any other education; he didn't have anything, so he sold his house to pay his doctor bills; he bought a little bitty trailer and a half-acre of land with what he had left, and he filed for disability. That was the only thing he knew to do.

He was sitting in his house the other day, out of food, and they were getting ready to cut his water off, and he didn't have any money. He was not a Christian; he did not know God. But he said, "I heard that place down there is good to people, and I want to go see if they'll pay my water bill." I told the deacon that I said to the man, "Sir, you may think that you came in here for your water bill, but you know God may be using everything that's happened to you in your life to get you to this place to make you realize you need Him. You need to be born again; you need to be saved."

I told the deacon that I paid the man's $32 water bill, and I gave him some food that he didn't ask for. I said, "There goes your brother in Christ right now because of a $32 water bill. Sir, now do you want me to spend your money on that man again?"

The deacon fell down and started crying. He said, "Ralph, I didn't know." The deacon wrote out a check that day and gave it to us.

That's the thing. People just don't understand this type of ministry and how God does use it. What happens sometimes with just a little bit. So what if someone sometimes takes advantage of us! Don't you know that whatever comes in here has been prayed over, and God makes us stewards of it? And God knows where it goes, and God is going to convict them. One day they will have to account to God for what they get through here if they do it in a wrongful way.

Miracles? Some of the greatest miracles happen here during Sunday morning services whenever we see the people come through that have been in jail, been on drugs, been on alcohol all their lives, and the power of God overtakes them, and He draws them to where they come up here to this altar, and they kneel and ask Christ to come into their life. That is one of the greatest miracles.

The other miracle is to see God start working with them once they get their life in order with Christ—to see Him taking them from being homeless to putting them into a home and getting them a job and then furnishing them with furniture and everything they need to get started back in life. So, a "Miracle on Fourth Street," as we call it, is a new start, new hope, and a new outlook at life. And yet, if people will accept everything that God gives them through here and go on with it, there's no reason for them to ever be back in the position they were in.

Two weeks ago, we watched two men receive the keys to their house—one had been living in the bushes behind the car wash, and the other had been living behind the Bean Pot restaurant. They got their keys; they've got jobs; and one of them is in college now.

The miracle in these men's lives is that they go from *hopelessness* to *hope*. Whenever they get a glimmer of hope and know their human worth and know that they can do something with their life, their whole outlook changes.

Whenever you see a mother who's got two babies tagging along, and their father just went off and left them, and they have nowhere to go—when you see them get into an apartment, and they have all the things they need, it's

90

wonderful. Then, they get involved in the churches in Crossville, and the pastors are coming over and accepting these people.

And more miracles. We kept seeing these brown spots coming from the roof. We got this company to come in here, and when they got down into it, they said the top was all rotted, and they needed to put a new layer of plywood down over it. So I went up and looked at, and sure enough, it was really rotted where the water had got to it, so we had to go ahead and do it. When they got through, the bill came to $8,000. I went into the office, and I said to Jim, "Jim, we've got to pray for $8,000!" And the next day, in the mail, we got a check for $8,000 from a lady in Florida. I don't know who she is, and I've tried to find out. I still have her name. But, the check she sent us from her will was for $8,000. God knew, and it just came together there to pay for our ceiling and roof. That's just the way it's been since we've been open.

God provides. (He even plans in advance...)

One day we went in, and we had run out of food. The pantry was empty. If I remember right, there may have been two or three cans of food. Me and my wife stood back there by a table, and I said, "Let's just pray." We prayed, and we asked God to replenish the pantry. Less than two hours later, a truckload of food came in. It was from a food drive that a church in Kentucky had for us. They brought the food in, and it filled the pantry right back up.

God provides. (Yep, and He plans in advance...)

I have tried so hard to tell people that God gives to his people not to hoard back or keep, but he gives it to us so we'll keep it supplied in the work of the kingdom. God says that if we'll keep busy about his work that he'll supply the needs. It is so simple—give and receive.

I took a few days off from here, and I got to go overseas on a mission trip to Rio de Janeiro with the Southern Baptists, and while we were there, we were painting this building, and I got to sharing with a lot of people how God is always on time with whatever we need. I said I've seen God do so much that there's no way I could ever deny him. The first service we had in that little old church, there were over thirty people who gave their hearts to Christ. Because when they see the power of God and know the power of God is real, they want to know him more intimately than what they do.

One of the hardest things I had to deal with when I became a Christian and started what we're doing here was having pastors saying they did not want the poor in their church. They told me not to bring them there. But to see that barrier coming down to where they're now coming out and helping the poor people and letting them come to their church, I can see God working through these churches. I believe this with all my heart—something in Crossville was almost dead.

Whenever we first opened up here, they asked if they could come over and do a dinner at night. They've been coming ever since we've been here. And that has transformed that church by letting the people in that church start utilizing their gifts that God's given them and seeing that they don't have to just sit in a pew, then go home; that they can work; they can do this, and they can do that, and whenever you've got a "can do" church, and the people realize they can do, they're going to get out and win more people to Christ. So, the poor more than likely see that they can be used. When the church members come in an see that the poor and indigent are people just like them, and it's not some stereotype of a homeless person they see on TV—that they are people, that they've got a soul, they've got personality, they've got something about them, most people fall in love with them. And, at one time they were afraid of them.

Children are the next generation of the church, and if we don't want them in church, then we're one generation away from not having a church.

When I was going to college, I traveled home every weekend, and I drove the church bus, and then went back to college—and on my route, I watched as five or six churches closed their doors. I asked God what is going on. It's coming to the place of apostasy—it's nearing the time for the Lord's return. The Bible says, "Where there is no vision, the people perish." Perishing is what's happening now.

I've never had much money, but I've really come to understand that everything I have belongs to God, and the more I give to the work of His kingdom, that is the only thing that I'm going to take to heaven with me. Anything that I hoard back, anything I keep back, is going to lay here when I'm gone.

An example, I had a lady who worked up here at a motel, and I'd go up there and witness to her a lot. I loved this woman; she was just a sweet woman, but she was a miser; she wouldn't spend a dime; she kept all her money back in a room.

She got sick, and the motel closed down, and she didn't have anywhere to live. So, me and my wife brought her into our home. The doctors told us she didn't have long to live; that she was going to die of cancer. So, we kept her as comfortable as we could and tried to be her family.

She had a little old car, an old Pinto, and I didn't have money enough at the time, and I would drive that little Pinto back and forth to work while she was staying at my house. The brakes went out on it, and I didn't have money to put new ones on.

That little old lady died, bless her heart; and they went over and found money hidden all over her house—in that room where she had been staying. We found out that she had over $150,000 in the bank.

Her son had never come to see her. Even though she would call him and beg him to come see her, he never came to see her. Well, he came up to see this lady after she died, and he never offered me and my wife a dime for keeping her and taking care of her. He got all her money out of the bank the next day—didn't even go to her funeral—and he took it to Chattanooga, where he lived. Less than eight months later, he was dead because he drank himself to death with that money.

So, there was a lady who went without—she ate hamburgers and beanie-weenies to save that money. She died, and the money was in the bank—didn't do her any good. Then, her son, a young man, got it, and it didn't do him any good either. Whenever we have money sitting back like that, really and truly, we're saying that we don't trust God; that we're going to keep it for ourselves. Then, we wake up one day—too late—because that money's laying there, and we're going to be accountable to God for it. Because it's still laying in the bank, not doing us any good and not doing Him any good. I wonder to myself how many people are in that position today.

We've always had our needs met here; we've never yet had to go out and beg and borrow. And, I just pray that we can keep trusting God to where He'll keep providing, so we don't have to do that. I have that faith, and I know my wife has that faith, and I know that we've got a lot of other people here who have that faith that God's going to build this new building, and we're going to have it up and occupied before the end of the year, and we're going to be able to put the people in there who need it because this is a place that's greatly needed.

It's not a place for someone to pat on the back and say, "Look what we've accomplished." It's accomplished for the work that God's called us to do, and the main objective of the whole thing is to lead men, women, boys and girls to Christ. To feed the hungry and clothe them and make sure they've got the things they need—to show them, number one, that we love them. A lot of times if you don't show people that you love them and how much you care, then they're not going to come listen to what you've got to say.

Since we've been here, I've personally got to baptize more than 5000 people in that little Baptistry there in the chapel. We had a baptism Sunday morning, I have another one tonight, for people who've been saved by coming through here.

That's why it's so important for people to understand this: I tell people that I'm the middle man to give what they don't want to the people who do need, but I'm also the middle man here in the work in the chapel because most of the people who come through here have been prayed for by somebody. They've been in the position that they know a little bit about church and about God. They've heard the gospel, so the seed's been sown in their heart. They come to the point where all the material blessings and possessions they had are gone. Then they come here, and I put a little water on the seed that people's

95

been putting in their hearts all through the years, and God brings it to fruition where they can get saved. So, it's just a watering and sowing.

A lot of people come through here, and they just get the seed sown. And, I pray that wherever they go from here, the water will be placed on them, because He says, "I will give the increase." Most of the people we see saved here have been on the fields. and they've had the seed sown in their hearts.

We've seen many prayers answered here. We had a gentleman come through here who stood up one night and said his best friend was in a Florida hospital dying; they said his heart was giving out. He was a young man, and they said if he couldn't find a heart transplant that he was going to die.

I said, "Let's just pray and believe that God is going to take care of his heart." So, we all started praying, and we prayed an intercessory prayer for that young man. A few days later, this gentleman who had asked for the prayer called me, and he said, "Guess what!" I said, "What?" He said, "The doctors went in to do the transplant surgery on my buddy, and they said his heart rate was so good they wanted to see what was going on. They gave him an x-ray, and said, 'He's got a brand-new heart!' They said his heart was good, and they used the transplant heart for another patient and let my friend go home."

That gentleman was back in here Sunday, and he was just praising God for His power. Intercessory prayer for the life of a man who needed a heart...

We've had people come through here who talked about cancer in their family. We've seen people survive cancer and become cancer-free, and we've seen some who

96

God healed ultimately and took them on home instead of curing them to stay here. I got to do their funeral, and people were being saved at the funeral through their testimony. Either way it goes, God has a purpose. God uses it through death or through life.

I guess the greatest miracle in the whole thing is how God can use a drunk, an alcoholic and a drug user—can change his life and put him back in a place where they can trust him and keep something like this going. One thing I've always said, "I know where I came from, and I know where I've been. I never want to put myself over or above anyone else or think I'm better than any, because I'm not. The minute you think you've done something by your own power and your own strength, and start patting yourself, that's when you will lose the power of God in your life. You can sense it, and if you ever get in that place, you'd better start repenting.

I have to say I repented a couple of times before I realized that I was saying, "Look what I've done." I can **never** say, "Look what *I've* done." It's always what *God* has done. He uses us for stewards. I like what Abraham said; "I'm a sojourner. This is not my home; I'm just passing through." When I die everything is going to be left here; the only thing I'm going to take with me is what I've given to other people.

If every Christian in the United States could understand that concept of what they have, do you know that we would never have to go out and ask for another dime. That's the way it's been since the beginning of Christianity.

I guess it's according to the person. I have a problem with fasting. I know that God honors fasting, but I have a problem with it because when I was growing up, I didn't know if I was going to have anything to eat or not.

So, I have fasted some, but not much because it's very, very hard for me to bring myself to that place of fasting. If you're raised very, very poor and you don't have anything, then you start being blessed, I can sense that person may have a hard time to even trust to give away some of their money. We want to make sure we don't do without. That's where we fail to trust in God. That's where I fail to trust in God—because God said He will take care of our needs. If we could just trust God with what we have, we could be much better people.

I went out today—and I won't call the young man's name—and you know I'm a collector of arrowheads. This young man had a collection of arrowheads that he wanted to sell for $500. I went out to look at them, and he had a beautiful collection. I began talking with him. His wife is in college, and he has a young boy with him there at home, and he said he just found out that he (the man) has an enlarged heart. He said, "If I don't sell these arrowheads for $500 today, I'm going to lose my place. I've got to pay my landlady today. Next week, I'm hoping to get to go back to work."

The Lord just said to me, "Give it to him. Don't take his arrowheads." In my greed, I wanted his arrowheads. This would be exploiting the poor; the boy needed the money. And his arrowheads were worth more than $500. I looked at the young man, and I teared up, and I said, "I'm not taking your arrowheads because God told me to give you the money."

I asked him, "Do you know Jesus Christ?" He just hung his head and said, "Yes, I know Jesus." I said, "You're my brother in Christ, and if I can't help you to keep your family and your house, I'm no good." I wrote him a check for $500 and gave it to him—and I didn't have it to give. But I gave it to him for one reason; I don't want to see that boy lose what he's worked for so hard. For $500, someone would take advantage of him. I believe it was James who said it is exploiting the poor to take from them in their time of need. When I left there, I knew that I had sowed a seed in his heart. He thinks everyone is against him, but he knows one thing—that there are Christian people in this world who will help you.

This is where James talks about "We have not because we ask not." And ninety percent of the people in a Christian church today won't ask. I remember back when I first started to church, on Wednesday night, we asked for needs in the church. People would say, "I need this, and I don't have it." So someone else would say, "Well, I have that, and I'm going to give it to you." You would be surprised at the people who have what the other people need but didn't know the other people needed it, and will give it to them free. Because we won't ask. But that's what the church is there for—to help our brothers and sisters.

You remember in the book of Acts on the Day of Pentecost what the people did—they sold their possessions and gave to the ones in need. They gave because they wanted to share their new life with others who didn't have. That's the greatest thing that Christ gives us is sharing, and if we can't share with other brothers and sisters in Christ, we need to look at our conversion.

We're now feeding a monthly average of 3500 meals. Since our doors were opened, (10 years in Feb 2011) that's between 40,000 and 42,000 meals per year. If you multiply that by nine years you get 378,000. We feed three meals per day.

Our food boxes themselves have increased tremendously in the last two years. We give out between 300-400 boxes a month to families who come in and tell us

99

their need. Before that, we were giving out about 150-200 boxes per month, so it's increased that much. We put enough food in a box to last them at least two weeks—based on the number of people in the family. We give them meat when we have meat; we give them canned food; we give them sweets; we give them breads and fruits—a big variety—spaghetti and macaroni—canned peaches and fruit. We know they'll be okay for two weeks.

And the miracles just keep coming...

Chapter 21

The Churches and Communities of Cumberland County

Some churches occasionally will provide a complete meal. Volunteers do come in to help with the food service and other chores that need to be done. As many as twenty to twenty-five volunteers are on a roster, and those volunteers call to tell them when they have some time available to help. Or, if a need arises, Connie, Ralph or Jim Young can call people on the roster to see if someone is available. They usually are—even if many of the volunteers are elderly retirees with limited physical capabilities.

In addition to helping prepare and serve the meals, volunteers also help with the landscaping and gardening. One volunteer, Vickie LaGow, helped Connie to create a beautiful Prayer Garden, which is right outside the entrance to the main building. Vickie also helps with the other landscaping around the mission. Ron Brining takes care of the financial business for the mission. Volunteers help with the building maintenance, yard maintenance, making donation pickups, and so forth. As Connie says, "God provides."

The mission now has seven paid workers, but all other work is performed by volunteers. This frees Ralph and Connie for overall supervision and to respond to needs as they arise.

One of the paid workers is Jim Young, the office manager. Frank Rector oversees the men's dormitory and does other jobs as needed, such as picking up donations. (Jim and Frank are ideal employees for a place like the mission because "they've been there too." They know what it's like to be held prisoner by weaknesses; Frank knows what a prison cell feels like. Their personal testimonies would make another book.)

Kim Lyles oversees the women's dorm. Both Frank and Kim live on the premises, which permits Ralph and Connie to go to their nearby home. Ralph and Connie theoretically have one day off per week—Friday—but they're usually there on Friday too. The Board of Directors sets all the salaries and benefits. Various community leaders and church leaders are on the Board of Directors.

In addition to their regular volunteer lawyer, Randall York, other local lawyers provide legal services and advice when needed.

In addition to the volunteers who come when they can, several doctors regularly provide a scheduled Medical Clinic from 5 p.m. to 7 p.m. every Monday and Thursday. See Chapter 19 for more about the Medical Clinic.

In addition to providing their medical ministrations, some of the doctors also donate gifts of personal items such as gloves, scarves, toboggans, coloring books and crayons at Christmas time.

One doctor's children earn money by performing chores at home, then they give this money to various charities on a monthly basis. Bread of Life is their charity for December. They give this to the mission to provide presents for the mission's "Pennies from Heaven" Christmas event. These same children also remind their mom (the doctor) when she is shopping at the grocery store, "Don't forget to buy some food for the mission!" In addition to helping the mission, she is deliberately teaching her children some important lessons of life—that not everyone has the same advantages of a good home and adequate resources. From the time they could walk, these kids have known the joy of giving, plus they are developing a great appreciation for their own loving family.

Incidentally, if a family wishes to receive a Christmas basket from the mission, they must first listen to the Story of Christmas. You might say the Christmas basket is a "gift that keeps on giving."

It is not easy to keep the mission functioning fully when its sole income is based on donations from local churches. The mission receives no federal or state funding because even though the mission is non-denominational, it is Christian. When you have thirty-nine or forty folks to feed three times a day, the food has to come from somewhere. When you have seven employees to pay, the funds have to come from somewhere.

A certain amount of the funds from churches is allocated to providing subsistence to those in need. When people cannot pay their rent or utilities because they've spent all their income on medicine, BOL will help them out. The BOL subsistence funds never last through the end of a month; in fact they only last the first few days of a month. This is one of the mission's biggest problems. We hate to keep putting out that sign that says, "No more subsistence funds are available this month."

Fortunately, from its inception, (actually prior to its inception) several Cumberland County churches pledged specific amounts to the mission, so it was guaranteed enough money to pay the mortgage and salaries. This money is doled out on a monthly basis. Unfortunately,

103

when it's gone, it's gone; the mission is out of funds until the following month.

The mission has a food bank, but certain foods are required on a daily basis, meaning they usually have an imbalance between the food on hand versus the food they need. When this happens, they phone their supporting churches and request a plea be made to the congregations for the specific items needed. They also sometimes let their regular volunteers know of the shortage. For example, the mission needs a great deal of peanut butter and jelly to prepare lunches for children to take to school. Churches and volunteers will get a "Peanut Butter and Jelly" call. As Connie says, "God provides." But…He uses His local citizenry to accomplish it.

The present mission kitchen is so small that they cannot have a dishwasher, and it will only accommodate one refrigerator and one stove—not nearly enough. Cabinet space is extremely limited. Two people working in the kitchen are in each other's way. The serving area is tiny. The dining area can only accommodate from twenty-four to thirty people at one seating.

Even though construction of the longed-for and much-needed expansion has now begun, they are already aware that it will not be enough. More land and more buildings are needed already.

* * * * * * *

Ralph and Connie hope this book will help to make people aware of the community's great needs, and that it will inspire them to enjoy the blessings of being part of the mission's work. And not just this community—but communities all over the country, because every community has homeless, destitute, hungry people who can be helped.

About the Author
(and a bit more)

Ralph Randall Reagan was born 6 September 1955, the seventh of ten children, in the small city of Crossville, Tennessee, which is about 100 miles east of Nashville.

At an early age, Ralph began stealing to get what he wanted, drinking beer at age nine because he could get away with it, and falling in with career criminals in his late teens.

Ralph had a miraculous conversion experience in prison. After many years of living the life of a drunkard and a criminal, facing death many times but miraculously escaping, Ralph now realized that life as a Christian offered many more rewards and better rewards. He soon felt called to the ministry.

Ralph had dropped out of school in the sixth grade as explained in the book. However, after becoming a Christian, with the help of members of Gideons International, who would later become good friends, and with moral support and financial assistance from his church in Crossville, Ralph was able to get his high school diploma through the GED program, and complete a college degree (bachelor's degree) at Clear Creek Baptist Bible College, Pineville, Kentucky, to become an ordained minister. He accomplished all that in three-and-one-half years. He was ordained by the First Baptist Church, Crossville, on 7 July 2004. He completed his master's degree in Biblical Theology in March 2008, and his Doctor of Theology in October 2009, from Slidell University, Slidell, LA.

In January 2001, with the help of First Baptist Church, Crossville, and other local area churches, Ralph's dream for helping those down on their luck became a reality—the Bread of Life Rescue Mission opened its doors.

The Bread of Life Rescue Mission is by no means a "flop house." They offer a safe haven for families or individuals while assisting them to find permanent housing and jobs. They teach and guide people in all aspects of a good life—from personal hygiene to personal responsibility to personal salvation.

The churches and individuals of Cumberland County pledged to donate money and food to support the ministry, and all have lived up to their promise. The mission receives no federal or state assistance.

Volunteers from all denominations can be found at any time at "BOL" helping with office administration, management, serving meals, performing maintenance, lawn maintenance, sorting through donations, or operating the medical clinic.

Ralph also has a prison ministry. He has more access to prisoners than most because of his background.

107

Now serving on the Community Resources Board of the Southeastern Tennessee State Regional Correctional Facility (STSRCF), Pikeville, he is inspiring the "powers that be" to expand their volunteer base to assist in providing inmates the resources needed to avoid recidivism. Volunteers must undergo a rigorous background investigation before being accepted.

The warden, Jim Morrow; deputy warden; chaplain, Gary Linebaugh; assistant chaplain, Bill Hall; Ralph and others from throughout the area are banding together to find people who can teach adults to read and write, how to open a checking account and balance a checkbook, vocational skills, other life skills necessary in today's environment, and to help them prepare for the GED.

The prison has a two-year curriculum teaching everything from fatherhood to fire fighting, from anger management to stress management, from reading to mathematics, from alcohol abstinence to drug abstinence, from personal hygiene to personal health, from how to seek a job to how to interview for one. They teach them to evaluate the cost of an item in terms of dollars, rather than "how many packs of cigarettes."

When people can find a job, support their families and cope with daily needs, they can become useful members of society instead of burdens to society. Without this, they will be right back in prison.

Statistics show that ninety-seven percent of the prison inmates will be released back into the community.[17] Because of this, the prison administrators and the community must work together to help the incarcerated become better citizens.

---

[17] Data obtained from the web site
www.state.tn.us/corrections/instituions/strcf.html.

This group was instrumental in getting a halfway house established in McMinnville, Tennessee, with Bill Hall as the manager. They now house eight persons at any given time.

Incidentally, the chaplain's services of STSRCF are provided to people of any religion. They provide equal services for Buddhists, Muslims, Christians, or any other that inmates represent.

Ralph is a fine-looking man who shows no sign of having lived such a hard and dangerous life. He is a man at peace with himself—at last. He spends his time now hunting arrowheads as a hobby and the souls of men as a profession. And, always, furthering his formal education.

Ralph has requested that the governor of Tennessee expunge his criminal record so that Ralph can attend law school. He feels that he then will be better equipped to help prisoners who have promise of "going straight." As of this writing (September 2010), all except one charge have been expunged, and he is hopeful that one will soon be expunged.

Hearing the name "Reagan" is no longer reason to cringe in disgust or fear in the city of Crossville, Tennessee. Bearing the surname "Reagan" is a source of pride and self-respect. Family members are now involved in law enforcement and a ministry to the homeless, as well as other legitimate pursuits.[18]

---

[18] On 8 February 2008, as the first edition of this book was being finalized for printing, Ralph's nephew, Matt Reagan, a police officer, was killed in a traffic accident. Matt's funeral procession was the largest ever in Crossville and Cumberland County. Uncle Ralph preached the funeral.

I, *even* I, *am* he who blots out your transgressions for my own sake, and remembers your sins no more.

Isaiah 43:25 (NIV)

Connie

This is her story
(and a bit more)

Connie Reagan has had a rough row to hoe all her life.

Due to the death of her father when Connie was small, Connie ended up being shuffled around to various places to live. It was not easy; in fact, it was downright hard. It left Connie feeling unloved and unwanted for many years.

Then, she met, fell in love with and married Ralph. And that turned out not to be easy either. Instead of "living happily ever after," life became worse in many respects. In fact, there were times when it was terrible.

Connie says that she and her children went to bed many, many nights wishing they had a bite of something to eat. The next morning, there still wouldn't be anything to eat. Even though she worked two jobs, she could not earn enough for everything. At times, when it was cold, she would put the babies into her bed, and she would lie on the floor beside them, waking the following morning to find her cover frozen to the floor because water crept into the trailer where they were staying.

She asked God many times to change Ralph's ways. Ralph was mean, vile and abusive when he would come home drunk—on those rare occasions when he even came home. Connie felt that she must have done something wrong, and God was punishing her; otherwise, she would not be having to endure such an existence. Many times, she was near the breaking point. Many times she prayed, "Lord, You can do this; I can't. I can't take anymore pain and heartache. Is it right that we have to live like this?"

In the early years, when Ralph was drinking and running around with unsavory characters, she took a lot of abuse from both him and his friends. They said all kinds of mean and cruel things to her. They would find any money she had saved and hidden away for groceries and go spend it on beer. Ralph taught the children to disrespect her. She spent years being miserable. Only her strong love for Ralph and her faith in God kept her going.

At one point, when Ralph was in a hospital near death, the doctor told Connie that "the next time he comes, it will be his last"—that she needed to be making arrangements. There she was with three young children and a drunken, criminal husband near death.

"When he told me that, I was broken in two. I took my three babies, and I walked out of there. I said, 'Lord, I cannot take this anymore. Either take him or change him. I've lived a life of pain and heartache, and I can't take it anymore.' Walking away from that hospital was one of the hardest things I've ever done. I loved him so much.

"But, I was determined that my babies would not grow up without Mama and Daddy, no matter what sacrifice I had to make. I was determined to keep them in a family environment. It was hard. My son would say, 'Mommy, when I grow up, Daddy won't hurt you anymore.' And, when Ralph was in prison, my girls used to cry out for their daddy. They had seen him shackled and taken away in a police car. It was hard. They loved their daddy, but they had learned that when he came in from a binge, they had to be quiet and let him sleep. They knew he did bad things.

"I gave my children all the love that I could. I taught them to love their daddy, not to hate him, even though they shouldn't approve of what he was doing."

Even after Ralph's conversion experience, Connie remained on her guard because she'd been hurt so much and disappointed so often. Even though she loved him with all her heart, she couldn't bear the thought that it wouldn't last. "God had to show me that it was real."

"When he backslid after losing three brothers back-to-back, it was like death to me. What did I do? Got down on my knees—because God had not one time given up on me. Without realizing the circumstances that were causing Ralph's problem this time, I asked God, 'Why? Why?' I said, 'I'm not going to be hurt anymore.'"

"When Ralph went to Florida for that year to try to get straightened out, I stayed home with the kids and worked. I did some things wrong. But, I had been hurt so badly—my husband, in his hour of despair, did not turn to either God or to me—he reached for the bottle instead.

"But then, God took over and fixed it. And, I've been blessed ever since."

113

Today, she and Ralph have a wonderful relationship. And, after Ralph's conversion, and getting their children through the "terrible teens," the relationship of both parents with their children has become great also.

As an example of the current relationships, when Ralph graduated from college, his son, Randall, embraced him and told him how proud he was of him. Ralph was moved to tears as he told Randall how proud he was of him, his son. Ralph said Randall was everything he wished he had been when younger.

The two daughters have long since forgiven Ralph for abandoning them when they needed him most, and they too now have good relationships. Each of the three children has two children, and they are raising them in Christian homes.

All of Ralph's and Connie's six grandchildren, whose ages range from sixteen to six, are well aware of Ralph's and Connie's mission. The older ones have accepted Christ. The younger ones are already following Christian principles as they enjoy helping those who are less fortunate. They even give their toys to Ralph and Connie to provide them to homeless or destitute children who have none. Ralph and Connie feel confident that these grandchildren will never go astray; they are very conscious of the need for Christian faith, hope and love.

Connie doesn't want anyone else to experience the pain and sorrow of sending her children to bed hungry. Connie herself knows what it is like to go to bed hungry— and she wants to ensure that no one has to do that.

BOL tries to help everyone in need, but they do draw the line at two things: you cannot stay there if you're drinking or on drugs.

114

To show people they're serious, Ralph and Connie have a zero tolerance policy. They routinely have the police come in with their drug-sniffing dogs. Both Ralph and Connie definitely do not want the mission to become a "flop house," and it will not. Most of the people who come to them for help are good people; they are just people who have lost their job, got behind on bills due to illness, have nothing left over after buying required medicine, have had their car break down while traveling, or have had some other stroke of bad luck.

Those who come to the mission know that they will find "tough love" there. They sometimes call Connie "The Warden" or "Big Mama." She laughs. "God needed a big woman for this job. I've been made fun of all my life, but now when people call me 'Big Mama,' they say it with love. Besides, with the love of the Lord that is in me, it wouldn't bother me anyway."

So, both Ralph and Connie have come a long way from their "roots." After many years of hardship and heartache, they've finally, with God's help, found their mission in life and peace with each other. Ralph's brown-haired, green-eyed lady loved him when he was extremely unlovable. And, God loved him when he was extremely unlovable. And, between the two of them, they saved a life that is now lovable—and is saving others.

Ralph had his conversion experience when he was about twenty-eight years old; he is now fifty-four. Almost half of Ralph's life was wasted, but the latter half has borne great fruit.

Connie knows now that this was their destiny. It isn't often that two people fall in love with each other the first time they meet, and so briefly at that, so it must have been destiny. Life still is not easy; they do not have wealth

115

or fame, but they have the peace of knowing they're helping God's children and, hopefully, preventing others from having to suffer as they did. Connie knows, from hard experience, that "life is what you make it."

"I've watched Ralph go from being this mean, vicious human being to a man that God has used to help so many. God took these two impossible lives and gave them possibility. And, I thank Him so much. I know that God kept His hand on me through all those bad years.

"I am truly blessed. I thank God for Ralph Reagan. I thank Him that Ralph's my helpmate. We're one. All that tug-o'-war that was between us for all those years is gone.

"A lot of people didn't think we'd make it. But, my God doesn't lie.

"My grandmother prayed for Ralph, Sonny and Bill. Sammie Selecman has prayed for Ralph ever since he was fourteen. She is now one of the mission's best volunteers. She's seen him from then until now and knows all the circumstances. She's seen the answer to her prayers."

Connie laments that, in spite of the numerous volunteers and churches who assist, thousands and thousands more in the community have no idea what the mission is or does. Or, what its needs are.

As an example of something other than meals and religious services, Bread of Life will assist people get decent clothing by coordinating with the Good Samaritans Thrift Shop. BOL provides a voucher good for three complete sets of outer and underclothing. They usually telephone "Good Sam" to let them know they're sending a person or a family. Likewise, Good Sam might phone BOL to tell them they're sending someone for food or other assistance.

BOL tries to help people find jobs. They help them save money so that they can rent an apartment or a house. They teach them personal hygiene and provide them with supplies such as soap, shampoo and toothpaste. Sometimes, travelers passing through experience breakdowns or other problems, and they come to the mission to get help. People can stay with them until they have another place to go.

As mentioned earlier, the Reagan grandchildren willingly offer their toys to the less fortunate. Perhaps they learned that from their grandmother Connie who also gives the clothes off her back—literally.

An example: One day while en route to Cookeville, TN, Ralph and Connie picked up a woman alongside the road. The woman was dirty and pitiful. She admired Connie's new shoes. What she didn't know, of course, was that Connie had waited a long time for those shoes to go on sale so she could afford to buy them. She had just bought them. When Connie looked down at the woman's pitiful feet that needed shoes badly, she immediately reached down, took off her new shoes and insisted that the woman take them.

As Connie is fond of saying, "God provides." It should be noted, however, that He usually uses us humans to fulfill His mission. The Gideons began the miracle, local churches and Christian friends nourished it, and the Reagans are two disciples who are fulfilling it. They have received, and they are giving. But—they could do more good if more people were aware of their work.

Ralph and Connie Reagan in front of the Bread of Life
Rescue Mission Chapel, which they founded

Ralph and Connie Reagan at the entrance to the Bread of Life Rescue Mission Office (Prayer Garden in the background)

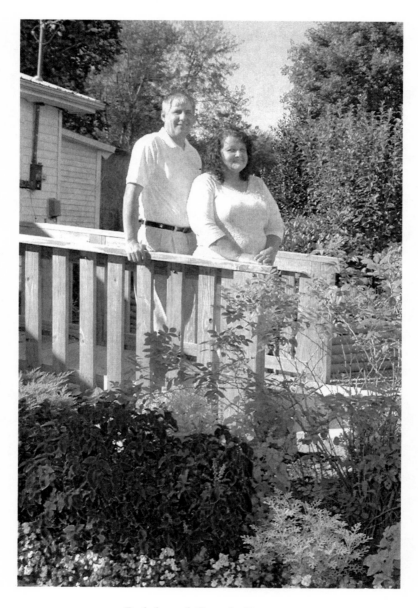

Ralph and Connie Reagan

121

Deaths in Juvenile Detention Facilities

As we go to press in 2008, more attention is being paid to deaths in juvenile detention facilities. Facilities throughout the United States are being investigated, and some of them already have been closed because of problems with staff and the way they treat the inmates. Others have greatly improved their operations by increasing salaries, re-training staff, and so forth.

The US Justice Department, Office of Justice Programs has published statistics in a variety of formats. These are available on the internet.

During the period 2001-2005, there were 356 deaths of juveniles in Tennessee facilities. Of these, some were suicides, some were homicides, some were natural or accidental, and a few were listed as "unknown."

Space does not permit a thorough analysis of the data available because it is voluminous. Go to http://www.ojp.usdoj.gov/bjs/ and then click the link for "Deaths in Custody."

President Bush's FY 2009 Budget includes $1 billion to assist states, communities and tribes combat the serious problem of juveniles who end up in detention.

The budget funds will be used to address the challenging problems of gun and gang violence, drug-related crimes, and the exploitation of children. Since much recent attention is being given to the problem of abuse in juvenile facilities, it is hoped that some of the funding will go to research and improve conditions.

(But, too late for Ralph's friend Raymond...)

Postlude
(By Collene Martin)

May 5, 2001, the Bread of Life Rescue Mission had her official coming-out party. Officials of the city, the mayor and the chief of police of Crossville were there. Pastors and deacons of First Baptist Church of Crossville were there, along with pastors and deacons of other area churches.

The dedication service was a time of blessing and gathering of those who had seen Brother Ralph at his worst, and now at his best, on his journey out of darkness into the light.

You could almost hear the thoughts and feelings of the people as they sat there watching the scene unfold. "Look at what you have done, O God, in the life of one man who was so full of wrongdoing. I sit here watching this, but You still do miracles in people's lives every day."

Some merely accepted the wonderment of it all and basked and bathed in the presence of the Holy Spirit. Some may not have realized the awesome moment at hand, but each one was there to support a man who had come far and had somehow touched their lives. Family, friends and co-workers watched in awe.

This day of dedication was a crowning culmination, and yet, it was a day of beginning. People had come from all over the Cumberland Plateau area, probably with various degrees of expectation. The excitement of the hour was electrifying. It showed forth the expectations of greater things to come. It was as if you were in the waiting room of a hospital delivery room. You could see that there were new babies about to be birthed into the kingdom, new Christians about to start a new way of walking in the Lord.

Souls would be changed in this place.

You could feel God's presence from the opening prayer to the closing. As Sister Connie sang "Amazing Grace," you could see the Spirit of the Lord touching the hearts of each person there.

This dedication service was merely a beginning. The curtain was about to rise on a massive collection of miracles to come.

As you listened, you heard how God had placed $100,000 into their hands to purchase the property.

You heard how Brother Ralph had petitioned God to find the right property that would be less than $100,000. You heard how God used a retired minister working in real estate, praying as he went, to find the right property—and finally finding it for $97,000.

Yes, there she is—the Bread of Life Rescue Mission—a beacon of hope to neighbors, the homeless, and the hopeless—a receptacle for the heart in need of Christ.

At the mission, a couple came by requesting food. They couldn't quite make ends meet. It was provided. A man needed medication, and a doctor was there to call a prescription in. He was one of the seven[19] doctors of the new free clinic. A woman who was a member of Fairfield Glade First Baptist Church was landscaping. Concrete had been poured for a new back porch. Showers had been installed for the men's dorm.

Life and excitement was in the air. Things were being accomplished.

A precious lady, also from Fairfield Glade First Baptist Church, brought ham, yams and deviled eggs, so

---

[19] Now many more doctors are volunteering for the Medical Clinic. Also, several more respond when needed.

124

they wouldn't have to cook supper. Brother Ralph had his nose in the refrigerator, excited about all the goodies brought. He was like a little boy filled with delight at all the wonderful things happening there that day and every day.

How could this happen here in the small, growing town of Crossville, Tennessee? How could there be beds, food and clothing for the needy coming from every direction, coming from some of the most unlikely sources? How could there be all this life and love showered on this little corner of the world? Only God could knit together such an intricate plan.

We saw fruit being produced when thirty-three souls were led to Christ and baptized at the Bread of Life Rescue Mission Chapel in the month of December 2001. Many other lives are being touched and changed daily.

Now, January, 2005, the number of souls saved at Bread of Life Rescue Mission is more than 800[20] since February 18, 2001, when the mission doors first opened, offering the "Bread of Life." The growth plans for the future of the mission are a 100-bed facility with a commercial kitchen. They're feeding the hungry bodies and the hungry souls.

In 2004, Brother Ralph's precious mother went home to be with the Lord. She had seen God move mightily in her son who had done so much to make her cry through the years, but her tears were dried. She had seen God's hand on the boy who had been such a problem.

Truly, when Brother Ralph accepted Christ, he was a treasure that Satan wanted to be kept hidden in the dark. But just look at God! He has put in the heart of one man a

---

[20] This number is now more than five thousand.

125

mighty work to be done for God's own glory. Because of the forgiveness of much, God turned on the great driving force of love.

Brother Ralph knows that only the hand of God has done all that you see before you. He also knows that there were those who told him some nineteen years ago that they would put him so far back in prison that he would never get out or see the light of day again.

It took two faithful servants, Gideons, men accustomed to giving the Word of God freely to all who would receive their Bibles, to reach one who would send ripples throughout this region. They were being obedient to His call. They did *not* see the many wonderful things God foresaw that could and would be accomplished through Ralph Reagan's life. These two merely did what they were called to do, which was to distribute Bibles.

However, it was not left at that. Earl Reagan had planted the seed, and Don Crace watered it as faithful brothers and friends. God knew that Ralph Reagan needed divine intervention and that great things would come from this special relationship that would be nurtured.

We are all called out of darkness, but Ralph Reagan heard and obeyed. He may not be perfect, but he is a man obedient and trusting God.

Thank you to all obedient servants who bear the name of Gideon, and to brothers and sisters in Christ throughout the world who share the Word of God and who live and die for Christ's sake.

I recently met an arresting officer, then Officer Danny Smith, now Pastor Danny Smith of Crab Orchard Christian Church. Brother Ralph and the Bread of Life Rescue Mission came up in our conversation, and it seems that Brother Danny was the arresting officer when Ralph

Reagan was arrested after his escape from Knoxville, just prior to his salvation experience. Danny experienced the old Ralph and the new Ralph. Praise God for saving and creating a new Ralph Reagan. Look at God's goodness.

It is no secret what God can do.
What He's done for others,
He'll do for you.
With arms wide open,
He'll pardon you.
It is no secret what God can do.

Stuart Hamblen was known as a hard-drinking man before he found Christ. It is said that his response to either John Wayne or Billy Graham commenting on the change in him was "It is no secret what God can do," and that person said, "You ought to write a song about that."

Thus was born, "It Is No Secret."

---

[21] Used for educational purposes only.

Mailing address for the Bread of Life Rescue Mission is:

Bread of Life Rescue Mission
281 W. Fourth Street
Crossville, Tennessee 38555

To purchase books, contact:

Miracle on Fourth Street Press
281 W. Fourth Street
Crossville, TN 38555
Telephone (931) 707-0503

Net proceeds of all book sales will go to the Bread of Life
Rescue Mission, a 501(c)(3) non-profit organization.

CPSIA information can be obtained at www.ICGtesting.com
Printed in the USA
LVOW122046141211

259385LV00002B/2/P